Immortal Summer

Immortal Summer

A Victorian Woman's Travels in the Southwest

The 1897 Letters & Photographs of Amelia Hollenback

Edited and Annotated by Mary J. Straw Cook

MUSEUM OF NEW MEXICO PRESS
SANTA FE

Caption text by Amelia Hollenback appears in quotation marks and is taken from her scrapbooks.

Cover: Verde Valley, Arizona; (inset) Grand Canyon.

Frontis: Thurber's Camp, Grand Canyon.

Photo page vi: Hollenback summer residence ("The Cottage"), Glen Summit, Pennsylvania, ca. 1880s.

Copyright © 2002 Mary J. Straw Cook.

All rights reserved. No part of this book may be reproduced in any form or by any means whatsoever, with the exception of brief passages embodied in critical reviews, without the expressed written consent of the publisher.

Project editor: Mary Wachs
Manuscript editor: Sarah Whalen
Design and Production: David Skolkin & Bruce Taylor Hamilton
Manufactured in China by C+C Offset Printing
10 9 8 7 6 5 4 3 2 1

Library of Congress Cataloging-in-Publication Data Available
Hollenback, Amelia, 1877-1969.
  Immortal summer : a Victorian woman's travels in the Southwest : the 1897 letters & photographs of Amelia Hollenback / edited and annotated by Mary J. Straw Cook.
  p. cm.
  Includes bibliographical references and index.
  ISBN 0-89013-402-2 (alk. Paper) – ISBN 0-89013-4003-0 (pbk. : alk. Paper)
Southwest, New—Description and travel. 2. Hollenback, Amelia, 1887-1969—Journeys—Southwest, New. 3. Women travelers—Southwest, New—Bibliography. 4. Indians of North America—Southwest, New—History—19th century. 5. Southwest, New—History—1848—Pictorial works. I. Cook, Mary J. Straw (Mary Jean Straw) II. Title.

F786.H76 2002
979'.02—dc21
                                              200206932

Museum of New Mexico Press
Post Office Box 2087
Santa Fe, New Mexico 87504

Contents

vii   PREFACE
The Hollenback Collection

1   INTRODUCTION

9   CHAPTER ONE
To Fort Leavenworth with Sweet Peas

22   CHAPTER TWO
There's Nothing Puritanical about Flagstaff

43   CHAPTER THREE
John Hance's Grand Old Cañon

59   CHAPTER FOUR
Punching the Breeze on the Rim

75   *The 1897 Photographs*

101   CHAPTER FIVE
Montezuma Had a Well and Castle in Arizona?

113   CHAPTER SIX
Oh, To Be an Acoma Cow

130   CHAPTER SEVEN
Snakes, Huggers, and Photographers at Hopi

151   BIBLIOGRAPHY

159   INDEX

Preface
The Hollenback Collection

—◆—

When Amelia Beard Hollenback died in 1969 at age ninety-two, two of her surviving great-nieces rescued, from the Hollenback residence in Brooklyn, a trunk filled with five generations of letters, diaries, journals, and memorabilia from the large Hollenback family. Included in this treasure trove was the story of the 1897 trip that is the subject of this book. From 1969 until 1981, the trunk remained locked and stored in the basement of a Manhattan apartment house, its historic contents known only to the family.

Amelia was the last of her generation to die, outliving her five sisters who lived to adulthood and three siblings who died in childhood. The Hollenback family home at 460 Washington Avenue in Brooklyn, New York, is also gone, demolished in 1983. The author's connection with this story began in 1971, when my husband and I purchased Amelia's house in Santa Fe (see page 145). Its contents proved to be a forty-year time capsule of her life in New Mexico, from the time she built it in 1932 until her death. As time passed, I began planning to write a biography of Amelia Hollenback. Growing up in Santa Fe in the 1940s, I recall riding my bicycle past the dark, lonely house dominating a small hill near today's St. John's College, and my early curiosity about the house and its owner never waned. In 1953 I drove my future husband past the seemingly uninhabited adobe and also spoke to my father, who, as an employee of the grocery store she patronized, had known Amelia Hollenback.

After moving into the house, I was greeted at the front door one day in 1972 by the late John Gaw Meem, who was Amelia's architect. When I asked him why she had built such a magnificent house, today an outstanding example of Pueblo revival architecture, yet never stayed in it for more than a few brief visits over thirty-seven years, he said, "Why don't you solve the mystery?"

Meem died in 1983, but he learned part of the answer to the Hollenback mystery on his deathbed. Too weak to read, he viewed a photographic story I had assembled to show him the results of my research on Amelia and her family. Meem always regarded the Hollenback house as one of his great architectural accomplishments; however, he gave much credit to Amelia whenever he spoke about her, though he never knew how she acquired her knowledge of Southwest architecture. The late art historian and author Bainbridge Bunting once related to me that she had made ninety-nine architectural changes in the original 1932 house plans.[1]

In the years following our move, my fascination with the enigmatic Miss Hollenback continued to grow, along with my determination to write about her. I began interviewing the few merchants in Santa Fe who had known her, such as Tony Taylor, owner of the Old Mexico Shop, and Charlie Kaune of Kaune's Grocery. I also interviewed three chauffeurs, two in Santa Fe and one in Pennsylvania. In 1977 a crucial door opened. Department-store magnate Stanley Marcus, a man I barely knew at the time, offered his valuable assistance in New York City. With Marcus's help I learned the names and addresses of Amelia's heirs. Her guardian and closest relative was Mrs. Dorothy Twyeffort Hubbell of Bedford, New York, who was her niece and the daughter of her half-sister, Josephine Hollenback Twyeffort. I wrote to Mrs. Hubbell of my desire to write her aunt's biography, and from that time on, the Hollenback family has generously assisted me in every way possible.

On February 8, 1982, came another crucial revelation. A letter arrived from Mrs. Elizabeth Twyeffort Drake, Josephine Twyeffort's daughter-in-law. She wrote, "I just went down to my cage [storage area] and opened a wardrobe trunk. You should see the contents." She had stored the trunk years earlier for her daughters, Trina and Susan, after Amelia's death and the settlement of her estate.

I immediately flew to New York, where Mrs. Drake graciously offered me her Manhattan apartment in which to spread out the coal-dusted treasure of five generations of letters, photographs, and diaries. She then left on vacation. After covering the furniture and floors with sheets, I donned a smock and mask and did not leave the apartment for seven days. At the end of the week, I knew I had solved the Hollenback Santa Fe mystery but had also found a new and significant chapter of women's history in the Southwest. The reason why Amelia never returned to Santa Fe after 1947 involved family deaths and financial responsibilities, complicated by the infirmities of old age—she was already seventy when she left New Mexico.

Every historian dreams of such a discovery, but at the time I was a professional musician, and even though I was planning to write a biography of Amelia, I did not think of myself as an historian. Nevertheless, it became apparent even to my musician's eye that the letters and photographs from the Hollenback sisters' 1897 trip to the Southwest should be my first research endeavor. Two large, heavy albums contained over four hundred photographs taken in Arizona and New Mexico on that trip. A friend and I carried the albums back to Santa Fe on the plane. From this extensive photographic record telling of her early Southwest trips, I was able to compile a history to present to John Gaw Meem before he died. The following year I drove to New York to pick up the remaining contents of the trunk. With the family's permission, the Hollenback Collection is now temporarily housed in Santa Fe.

The saga continues to unfold with ongoing research. Another manuscript is in progress on the building of the Santa Fe house, including letters exchanged between Amelia Hollenback and John Gaw Meem. In addition, José Ronquillo, her one-time chauffeur, saved all his letters from Amelia throughout the almost thirty years he lived in her house as its caretaker.[2]

Adventure is always a part of discovery. A New York City cabdriver will never forget the experience of a strange woman stuffing every corner of his cab, including its trunk, with boxes and tied bundles, racing to the New Jersey entrance of the Holland Tunnel, and unloading it all into a waiting car with a New Mexico license plate. Fearing city traffic, I had parked in New Jersey. As we drove to the rendezvous point, I told the cabdriver some of my Hollenback adventures. Dumbfounded, he said, "Lady, no one will ever believe this. It's as good as an Agatha Christie mystery!" Knowing Amelia's love of Dorothy Sayers and Agatha Christie mysteries from the library left in our home, I felt she would have appreciated the cabbie's humor. But even more adventure was in store.

Later, in 1983, I made a pilgrimage to Amelia's grave in Wilkes-Barre, Pennsylvania. The Hollenback Cemetery there occupies a rolling knoll overlooking the Susquehanna River. Here rest several generations of the once powerful family that played so significant a role in Pennsylvania history during the eighteenth and nineteenth centuries. Near the cemetery, an abandoned coal breaker stood silent guard, its conveyor for large chunks of coal a skeletal reminder of the industry so closely linked to the Hollenback name, now all but forgotten.

I received directions to the cemetery from Wilkes-Barre's Wyoming Valley Historical and Geological Society, which had as one of its founders John Welles Hollenback, Amelia's father. Massive, black-painted iron gates announce the name "Hollenback" at the entrance on River Road. Once amid the groomed grass and tombstones on the most prominent section of the knoll and fighting swarms of gnats, I was immediately surrounded by Hollenback graves.

I had brought a handful of New Mexico earth to sprinkle on Amelia's grave. The pink, rocky soil came from the hill called San Estevan on which her house was built; from a small plateau, she often watched the myriad sunsets over the Jemez Mountains. Like Arizona's Grand Canyon, it had been a place of peace and solitude for her. Gray, weathered pieces of a carved and partially rotted wooden bench found on the hill now comprise a prized table in our home. Standing beside her grave, I thought Amelia somehow might have approved of the new occupants of her much-loved house.

In an intriguing coincidence, near the towering tombstone of Matthias Hollenback and that of his great-granddaughter Amelia, I found a smaller one with my maiden name, Mary J. Straw, and "Born Dec. 6th 1841–Died July 28th 1900" engraved on it. On inquiring about this woman at the historical society, much to my surprise I was told that she had lived next door to the Hollenbacks. Later, while going through the memorabilia from the trunk, I discovered that the woman named Mary J. Straw not only lived next door in Glen Summit, a summer retreat near Wilkes-Barre where they often stayed, but sometimes lunched with them. Several hand-painted luncheon place cards in the Hollenback Collection bear that name, attesting to yet another unusual connection between us.

Back in Santa Fe, as I continued my research and explored the contents of the trunk, I learned a great deal about the Hollenbacks' life in Brooklyn and Glen Summit. The story of Amelia's long attraction to the Southwest and its cultures unfolded; it apparently established deep roots during the 1897 trip. Before José Ronquillo, her longtime caretaker, died in 1984, I interviewed him about his reclusive employer. He had worked for her from the early 1930s until her death in 1969.

Among the many reminiscences he related about Amelia, whom he affectionately called "Holly," was that of her frantic final departure from Santa Fe in 1947. Eternally tardy since childhood, she had her days and nights reversed, often reading mysteries most of the night, then sleeping until two o'clock or so the next afternoon. On this occasion, when she at last emerged through the Spanish Colonial front door, José was forced to exceed the speed limit to reach the train station, some fourteen miles away, on time. As the large black Cadillac pulled into Lamy, New Mexico, the train was already moving away. For the next sixty miles, they pursued it on a wild, eighty-mile-an-hour chase through winding Apache Canyon between Lamy and Las Vegas, New Mexico, the next stop for the eastbound train.

Seconds after arriving at Fred Harvey's Casteñeda Hotel—also the train station in Las Vegas—José helped Amelia out of the car, handed her luggage to the porter, and waved goodbye. With reservation, she reached out to shake his hand for the first time since they had met some twenty years earlier. Heretofore, her upbringing had prevented any sort of physical contact with male employees, in spite of the youthful promises of breaking Victorian barriers that she had made in her 1897 letters. They never met again in New Mexico.

In 1956, Ronquillo rode the train to New York to talk to Amelia about making sorely needed repairs on the house. The roof was leaking, among other things. Her mud house, which she could never bring herself to sell during her lifetime, though there were one or two opportunities, quite simply was washing away from neglect. When he arrived at the Hollenback home in Brooklyn,

Amelia came to the beveled-glass door and stared vacantly at José. She no longer recognized her caretaker and refused to open the door. He took the next train back without saying a single word to her. According to her death certificate, Amelia suffered from cerebral arteriosclerosis in her last decade, a condition that progressively affects mental capacity.

An added dimension to this intriguing tale concerns Amelia's long and enduring relationship with the Tesuque and San Ildefonso Indians of New Mexico, who believe that I was "chosen" to tell her story. Finding the tombstone with my name in the Hollenback Cemetery, they say, was her way of telling me this.

Whatever the explanation, the intersection of my life with that of Amelia Hollenback's—from a childhood fascination to owning her Santa Fe home and being the custodian of her history in the Southwest—has been a great adventure for me. I have come to know her well, I think. The letters and photographs from the 1897 travels from Kansas to Arizona and New Mexico reveal her and Josephine's most intimate thoughts, even though they probably never intended for them to be read publicly.[3] More than a century later, we can revel in the enthusiasm, intelligence, and sheer pluck of these young Victorian women during their "immortal summer."

Notes

1. See Bunting, *John Gaw Meem*. The John Gaw Meem Archive of Southwestern Architecture, including the Ansel Adams photographs of the Hollenback house made in 1933, is held by the University of New Mexico General Library, Center for Southwest Research, Albuquerque.

2. A portrait of José Ronquillo, of Mexican and Tarascan Indian descent, presently hangs in the lobby of La Fonda Hotel in Santa Fe today over the chair he often occupied through the years. This handsome, mustached fellow was always in demand for small parts in movies filmed in the area.

3. All materials from the 1897 trip cited here are in the Hollenback Collection, Santa Fe, in the author's custody.

Introduction

Lord Curzon of Kedleston, a member of the prestigious Royal Geographical Society of London dedicated to the advancement of discovery, once ranted that "the genus of professional female globetrotters with which America has lately familiarized us is one of the horrors of the latter end of the nineteenth century."[1] Undoubtedly, Lord Curzon's statement touched a delicate nerve at 460 Washington Avenue, Brooklyn, New York, home of the six Hollenback sisters—Emily, Eleanor, Anna, Josephine, Amelia, and Juliette—all avid "female globetrotters of America."

Lord Curzon had opposed the admission of Isabella L. Bird, author of *A Lady's Life in the Rocky Mountains*, and fourteen other women to the Royal Geographical Society in 1893. He doubted their capability to contribute geographical knowledge, adding "their sex and training rendered them equally unfitted for exploration." The women were denied fellowship by a vote of 172 to 158, although Bird was later accepted. Lord Curzon considered women's emancipation the "fashionable tomfoolery of the day," but members of London's New Vagabond Club, at their annual dinner in 1897, heard a different message delivered about women: that no six centuries in England had produced so many eminent women as the last sixty years during the reign of Queen Victoria.[2]

Despite Lord Curzon's view of women travelers, and for reasons unknown, the year 1897 produced a wave of camera-carrying tourists to the American Southwest. Among the tourists from the East were two young and eager Hollenback women from Brooklyn. Though world travelers, they knew very little about Arizona and New Mexico, territories far west of the Hudson River they knew so well. The trip west meant that the two half-sisters, Amelia and Josephine, had to abandon their usual European summer holiday at a time when their New York friends would be sailing to London for the royal festivities of Queen Victoria's Diamond Jubilee. Thus in the summer of 1897, the queen, laced with stoic and bosomy vigor, would celebrate without two of her devotees, the Misses Hollenback. They chose instead to explore their own Southwest, snakes and all.

With newly purchased cameras in hand, Amelia and Josephine, called Minna and Jo by their family, boarded a train for Flagstaff, Arizona Territory, to expe-

Josephine Woodward Hollenback, ca. 1897.

rience what remained of the Wild West and to photograph what they believed to be a dying culture, that of the Pueblo Indian. The girls were doing what they did best—traveling to a distant place, taking photographs, keeping journals, and writing letters home about their adventures. Their three-month summer holiday to the Southwest fulfilled a long dreamed of excursion. They yearned to see the greatest of American natural wonders, the Grand Canyon of the Colorado in Arizona Territory, and to visit Indian pueblos and cliff dwellings in northwestern New Mexico Territory.

To prepare for the trip, Minna had spent her Easter vacation from Adelphi Academy in Brooklyn gathering information at the Smithsonian Institution in Washington, D.C., where a scale model of Arizona's Montezuma Castle was available. But no plaster-of-paris cliff dwelling could compare to the thrilling climb up five stories of sun-bleached ladders clinging to the face of an Arizona cliff. Nor could words describe a silent sunset on the rim of Grand Canyon.[3]

Indeed, few women traveled to the Southwest in 1897 expressly to camp out-of-doors, but in order to visit many of the Indian pueblos and ruins or Grand Canyon, camping out was necessary. Even fewer women tourists carried a camera, tripod, and the heavy, fragile glass plates required for making photographic exposures. The combination of camping and photographing during the nineteenth century demanded intelligence combined with stamina, two traits not often attributed to Victorian women by their male peers. Despite all prejudices inherent to the era about their gender, however, Minna and Jo Hollenback proved indomitable in their quest for adventure and, above all, knowledge.

The thirst for new experience constituted only part of their legacy as daughters of the wealthy John Welles Hollenback, who continually encouraged them as though they were sons; he had sired two boys but they died in childhood. Friends once said to the girls' mother, "What noble things you and Mr. Hollenback are doing for your daughters—worth more to them educationally than almost anything else which you might plan for them."[4]

In Brooklyn, the three-story Hollenback home was a hub of church and school activities. Social calls were formally made and received, announced by engraved calling cards. During the warm, humid summer days, however, the Hollenbacks were invariably traveling. Family members not globetrotting spent time at a favorite mountaintop retreat called Glen Summit, among the Pocono Mountains in Pennsylvania. The Hollenback summer migration to their multistoried, ten-bedroom clapboard house near Wilkes-Barre required one railroad car to transport family and servants, and another car for luggage, ponies with carts, linens, and canning jars.

Once in the invigorating woods of Glen Summit, the Hollenback women looked forward to summer teas, luncheons, and more formal dinners with delicately painted place cards at the table. Afternoon lawn parties with friends and neighbors included badminton, with the women wearing long tennis skirts. Hikes, picnics, and church socials were especially popular with the younger set. For occasions such as birthdays, Russian dancing bears delighted linen-frocked guests gathered on the large lawn.

Amelia Beard Hollenback, ca. 1897.

John Welles Hollenback (1827–1923) had moved his growing female brood away from the smoky and turbulent atmosphere of the coal mining industry in Wilkes-Barre to the sea-washed air of Brooklyn sometime before 1877, the year of Amelia's birth. His first two wives, Anna Elizabeth Beard (1835–1864) and Josephine Woodward Ferguson (1835–1872), had died at age twenty-nine and thirty-seven, respectively. His third marriage, which lasted forty-four years, was to Amelia Beard (1844–1918), a sister of his first wife.[5] Hollenback fathered nine children in all: seven girls—one by the first wife and three each by the second and third wives, including Josephine and Amelia. One of the daughters also died in infancy, as did the two sons from the first marriage.

The Hollenbacks were descended from generations of distinguished statesmen, scholars, and moneymakers. Their name in northeastern Pennsylvania equaled that of Rockefeller in New York, with one critical difference: no male Hollenback heir survived to perpetuate the name and financial dynasty.

The Hollenback family genealogy reads like a who's who from the pages of eighteenth- and nineteenth-century American history. John Welles Hollenback was born John Roset Welles in 1827 to Charles Fisher Welles and Eleanor Jones Hollenback. His father was a cousin of Gideon Welles, Abraham Lincoln's secretary of the navy, whose diaries were a major source for author Carl Sandburg's biography of Lincoln.[6]

Although his grandfather, George Welles, had graduated from Yale University in 1799, John Welles attended Athens Academy in Athens,

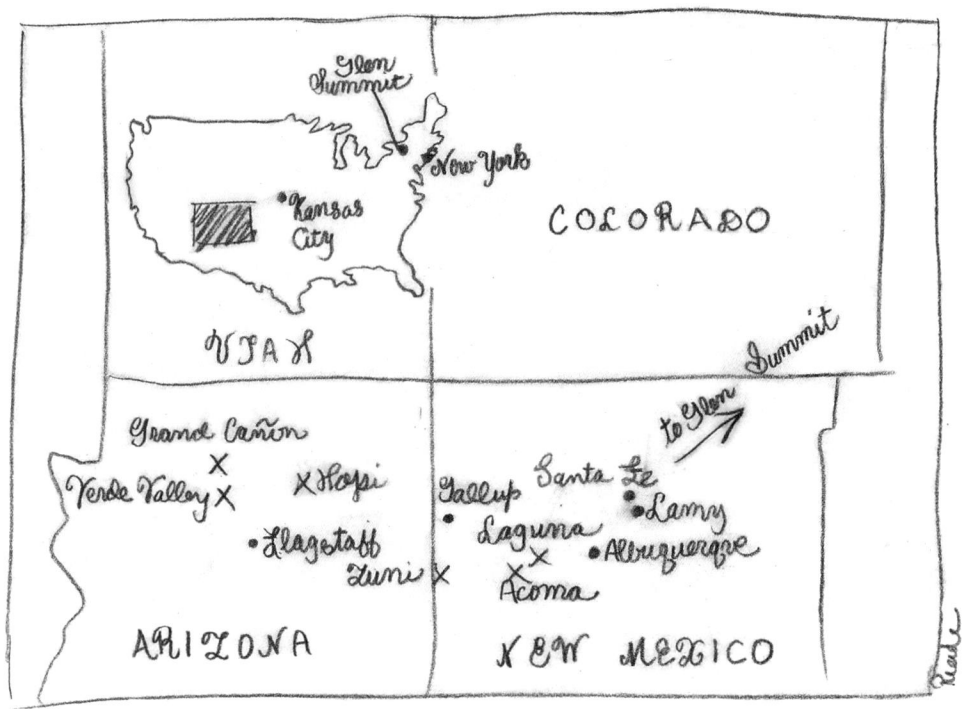

The 1897 travels of Amelia and Josephine Hollenback.

Pennsylvania. His maternal and paternal ancestors included the Pynchons (from William Pynchon, one of the original patentees of the Massachusetts Bay Colony and a founder in 1636 of Springfield, Massachusetts), the Holyokes, the Hollisters, the Talcotts, and the Welles (from Thomas Welles, the fourth colonial governor of Connecticut), all of whom were among the earliest settlers of Massachusetts and Connecticut.[7]

In 1862, at age thirty-five, John Welles legally adopted his mother's maiden name at the request of his wealthy but childless maternal uncle, George Hollenback, who recognized his nephew's business acumen. Until that time, John had been a schoolteacher, managing the family estate in Wyalusing, Pennsylvania. After entering the many Hollenback enterprises, he became an astute businessman over the years. Seldom at home, he commuted regularly—between Wilkes-Barre, the seat of the Hollenback financial empire, and Brooklyn, the family's residence. Even though he had lost two wives and three young children by 1872, there is evidence that he and his third wife and six daughters enjoyed many happy years together. Both parents seemed to have been actively involved with the girls' lives, encouraging their interests and education and taking trips together to many places.

The third Mrs. Hollenback's full name was Amelia Beard Hollenback; her namesake daughter later added a "Jr." after her name. The mother evidently

A birthday party for Amelia Hollenback given at San Ildefonso Pueblo, ca. 1935. Amelia is on the right; potter María Martínez, back row, third from right; Blue Corn Calabaza front row, fourth from left.

believed there was a great deal more to a nineteenth-century woman's life than marriage alone, for she penned a poem in the front of her address book, adding her own sentiment at the end:

> A maiden's wishes are but three,
> O'er all the world where'er she be
> To handsome grow, and have a beau
> And to the bridal altar go. *Not so!!!*

The Hollenback women were intelligent, curious, and adventuresome. They took great care, nevertheless, to research any unknown area to which they might travel. Traveling to the American Southwest in 1897 was considered a bit more risky than a trip up the Nile River in Egypt that sister Anna had made in 1894 with her camera, or a steamer trip to Alaska that nine-year-old Amelia had taken with her parents in 1886. Propriety and safety concerned the single woman traveler of the nineteenth century, although there were exceptions such as the numerous spunky but often naive women who headed for the Alaska Klondike in 1897.

"You will be safer in Arizona than on the streets of New York," wrote author and Southwest proponent Charles F. Lummis to twenty-year-old Amelia. In preparing for their trip, she had written to the editor of *St. Nicholas Magazine*, Mary Elizabeth Mapes Dodge, asking her to forward a letter to Lummis, who had walked from Ohio to California in 1884 and visited Grand Canyon in 1892

Hollenback family Brooklyn residence (460 Washington Avenue, now demolished), 1941. Tesuque Pueblo Indians were in New York as participants in a Museum of Modern Art program.

and 1895, writing about his adventures and first coining the phrase "See America First." Numerous articles by the peripatetic Lummis had appeared in *St. Nicholas*, a popular nineteenth-century magazine for young people. An enthusiastic reader of Lummis articles, Amelia cautiously inquired about the safety of two single girls alone in the West. His reply was encouraging and full of useful suggestions.

Los Angeles, Cal.
May 18, 1897

Dear Miss Hollenback:

There is no reason on earth why two American girls with sense enough to care for the Southwest should not see all they wish of it . . . and while you will not find all the comforts any fat-wilted person can get in a hotel, neither will you meet any hard-ships my wife and little girl cannot enjoy.

By all means go to the Grand Cañon, and take at least three days from Flagstaff. By all means go also to Acoma, the pearl of Pueblos. Stop at Laguna (and take time to see that young Pueblo, founded 1699). Get Mr. Kirsch [sic] to take you over to Acoma, about a 16 mile drive. Have him take provisions and blankets and stay over at least one night in Acoma. See the town and go down the trail southeast of the church and see if you are good for the trail nearly in front of the church. Go around as much as you can of the foot of the cliff. Go to the reservoir on the south mesa. Explore all you can, for you could not exhaust the place in a month.

Coming back from Laguna, stop at Isleta. Call on the priest, Father Docher, if you speak French. Find Manuel Carpio and get his daughter Felicita to accompany and interpret for you in the town.

For the Petrified Forest, arrange from Holbrook with Adam Hanna at Adameda, as you go West. Or you *can* go from Holbrook.

There are small room cliff-dwellings 8 miles from Flagstaff; if you wish a better one (a communal cliff-house), go from Flagstaff to Ash Fork and Prescott by rail, thence by conveyance to old Camp Verde, Montezuma's Well and Castle and the Natural Bridge. There is nothing in any of these trips you need shrink from. In most places it will do you no harm to say I sent you.

Wishing you the "good hunting" your American spirit deserves, I am

Sincerely yours,
/s/ Charles Lummis[8]

The Lummis letter to Amelia became an itinerary for the sisters, but he did not mention the Hopi Snake Dance, which all tourists to Arizona Territory were eager to witness. In following his suggestions, Minna and Jo Hollenback would experience adventure enough to last a lifetime—and perhaps longer.[9]

Notes

1. Zetland (Earl of Ronaldshay), *Life of Lord Curzon*, 1:195.

2. "Saturday Review of Books and Art," *New York Times*, June 26, 1897, 7.

3. Montezuma Castle is a cliff dwelling in the Verde Valley of north-central Arizona, so named because early visitors erroneously believed it had been built by the Aztecs of Mexico for their emperor Montezuma. Barnes, *Arizona Place Names*, 351. See Chapter 5.

4. Mrs. JWH to husband, Dec. 17, 1897, HC.

5. Hollenback genealogy courtesy of Virginia Welles; Mrs. Welles is a Hollenback from both sides of her family.

6. See Niven, *Gideon Welles*, 15; Sandburg (*Abraham Lincoln*) mentions Welles many times in his monumental biography.

7. Harvey and Smith, *A History of Wilkes-Barre, Luzerne County, Pennsylvania*, 5:181–83.

8. CFL to ABH, May 18, 1897, cited in JH to father, May 23, 1897, HC. Harvard-educated Charles F. Lummis was a frequent contributor to *St. Nicholas: An Illustrated Magazine for Young Folks*, published by the Century Company, New York. From Dec. 1891 to Oct. 1892, *St. Nicholas* published a six-part serial on Arizona by Lummis that later appeared as a book, *Some Strange Corners of Our Country*. Lummis wrote *A Tramp across the*

Continent in 1892 describing his 1884 trek across the Southwest. His greatest contribution in promoting the cultural heritage of the West was establishing the Southwest Museum in Los Angeles in 1907.

9. Acoma, Laguna, and Isleta are Indian pueblos not far from the railroad in northwest and north-central New Mexico. Historians have assigned Laguna three founding dates, 1697, 1698, or 1699, but July 4, 1699, is when the pueblo officially submitted to Spanish rule. *Handbook of North American Indians*, 9:187, 438. Math Kirch, a saloonkeeper and the wagon driver Lummis mentioned, and his wife Piedad are listed on the 1900 U.S. Census, Valencia Co., for the village of San Rafael, near Laguna, N.M. The Rev. Antonine Docher was the priest at Isleta from 1891 to 1926 and was noted for his architectural transfiguration of the church there to suit his French taste. Kessell, *Missions of New Mexico*, 219. Manuel Carpio and his wife Lupe are listed in the 1900 U.S. Census for Isleta Pueblo, south of Albuquerque. Adamana is a contraction of the name of Adam Hanna, who owned a ranch on the Rio Puerco near the Petrified Forest in Arizona. The station, established by the Santa Fe Railway around 1890, became a railroad stop for tourists visiting the Petrified Forest, although it was little more than a house or two in the desert. Hanna later sold his ranch and moved to Farmington, N.M., where he died. In 1879 Camp Verde was established in Arizona's fertile Verde Valley; the army stationed soldiers in the area as early as 1866 to fight the Yavapais and Apache Indians. Montezuma Well, a short distance from the prehistoric cliff dwelling called Montezuma Castle, looks like a volcanic crater filled with water but is in fact a limestone sinkhole caused by the collapse of an underground cavern. Though the castle and well are separate, both are part of today's Montezuma Castle National Monument in Verde Valley, Arizona. The Natural Bridge (now in Tonto Natural Bridge State Park), which spans Pine Creek in Verde Valley, is approximately five times larger than the better-known Natural Bridge in Virginia. Barnes, *Arizona Place Names*, 3, 109–10, 351, 360–61.

CHAPTER ONE

To Fort Leavenworth with Sweet Peas

———◆———

In the fall of 1897, after the memorable trip to Arizona and New Mexico Territories, Minna Hollenback dropped out of Adelphi Academy in Brooklyn because of what she described as a "clouded brain." Mrs. Hollenback wrote to her husband in December that year: "Even Minna in her enforced withdrawal from her loved pursuits, has the past rich in experiences of travel to live upon. The Arizona interests will never pale."[1] The impact of her adventures—and most of all the Pueblo Indian culture—would last a lifetime for the young woman.

Minna was profoundly influenced by her and Jo's visit to the Southwest. Her emotional and psychological change was apparent a year later as she recalled those unforgettable moments and attempted to write an expanded version of the trip from her meticulous notes. Even though she loved to write, it proved to be an uninspired project, however, covering only three and a half small pages in the back of her expense diary.

Commenced May 24, 1898

I am going to note down a brief diary of Jo's and my last summer's trip, as I naturally remember more than I would later.

June 1, 1897. Tuesday: Jo and I left home by the Black Diamond express at noon today, intending to spend about six weeks in New Mexico & Arizona. Mama & Nan came to the train to see us off, but were not allowed to pass beyond the ticket gate. Louis T. [Jo's future husband] & William our coachman, were allowed to board the train, as they were men. Great jokes about "no admittance to passengers' families." They (our family, Mama & Nan; Julie was in school) stood peering through the bars à la Charlotte Corday, & we stood on the "black platform" and waved to them as the train moved out.[2]

We had lunch on the dining car. We expected to feel as triumphantly joyful as a brass band on parade, but it was our most homesick day.

There was a thunder shower in the afternoon, with the most beautiful effects of light & cloud on the soft young leaves. I never saw the western part of New Jersey look lovelier.

At Glen Summit Mabel [a friend] stood on the platform waving a flag. She afterwards wrote that she heard me squeal. I didn't know I squealed, but if it carried above the roar of the train no wonder the other passengers smiled.

Papa, Lewis, Emily & Pud [a sister and family], Cousin Annie B. & Ellen & Ned [more family] met us at the Wilkes-Barre station, and we had a few minutes' talk. Pud brought me some P.K.[Pocket Kodak] photographs from Mabel, and Emily brought us each flowers. As Mama & Nan had each given both of us flowers, Ned L. [another boyfriend of Jo] had sent some more to Jo, and Louis had brought her a 2 lb. box of Huyler's [chocolates], we felt pretty well supplied with the necessaries of life; especially when on opening some packages Nan had put in our satchels we found two toy pistols with sketches showing us how to use them in the wild and woolly West.

Also a remarkable poem describing our *true* adventures. At about 10 p.m. we reached Buffalo & were transferred to the Chicago train. A dress suit case, a telescope, two satchels, two cameras, one case of plates, one tripod, one field glass, two umbrellas, box of candy, all those flowers, a porter and two lone girls make quite an imposing procession. Glad to get into our berths. Went to sleep with an S.P. [special?] feeling because I saw the Niagara rapids as we passed over them, a thing I had once before laid awake two or three hours to accomplish and missed it after all.

Wednesday, June 2. Began to-day in a bright, energetic, up-with-the-lark manner by sleeping just long enough to let the dining car come and go, and with it our breakfast. Jo waited for me and so didn't have any either. All very well for me but hard on Jo.

We got the porter to bring us two glasses of milk apiece at the next station, and had a good deal of fun over our five-minute square meal.

We had made a good many plans about calling on Miss B. [a friend], going to Huyler's [for more chocolates], etc., between trains in Chicago; but they were all frustrated. It poured steadily all the afternoon, so we had lunch in Dearborn Station (funny underground place, that restaurant), then bought magazines & sat in the waiting-room till train time; thankful that it was Wednesday & we could catch the California Limited at six-something, instead of waiting till after ten for the daily train.

Thursday, June 3. Arrived in Kansas City in time to do some needed shopping and take quite a long trolley ride before having lunch at the Midland Hotel. Smokiest city I ever saw, but not bad, for all that. (Kansas City, excuse this tone of patronage.) Nearly disgraced ourselves at lunch because our colored waiter *would* fan us all the time with a slow & pompous dignity that was too much for us. Jo saved the day by making a series of mild & pointless jokes at which we could both laugh. And we did! After lunch I wrote a letter to Juliette & Jo, one to some other member of the family, then we took the train for Leavenworth. We are to spend a few days at Fort Leavenworth with Mrs. Stevens, whose husband is studying in the officers' school there.[3]

Here, Minna's diary abruptly ends. Fortunately, the romantic and descriptive letters to her family the previous summer detail the adventures of a young Victorian girl on her first trip to the West. In her first letter, Minna vividly described Kansas City and Fort Leavenworth, which surely kindled a melancholy emotion in her father. He had taken a train west through Kansas to Colorado twenty-five years earlier, to recover from the sudden death of his second wife, Jo's mother. Apparently, travel was an important part of the Hollenbacks' lives and was made possible by the family's wealth.

In the late eighteenth century coal was discovered under Hollenback land in Pennsylvania, and anthracite formed the basis of the Hollenback fortune during the nineteenth century.[4] Durham boats on the Susquehanna and Delaware Rivers were used first to transport the family's mercantile goods from Philadelphia and Baltimore to Binghamton, New York, and water also powered their paper and lace mills.[5] Later, the railroad provided for business and travel, linking their sense of adventure to the rhythm of clicking rails.

Leaving Brooklyn for distant vacations usually meant leaving behind a cherished member of the family. In June of 1897 it was Juliette, the youngest, who remained in school at Adelphi Academy. Minna and Juliette, born four years apart to the third Mrs. Hollenback, were sisters of like humor and particularly close. Sixteen years earlier in 1881, upon Juliette's birth in Geneva, Switzerland, precocious four-year-old Minna was taken on a shopping trip for her new sister to a Geneva toy shop, where she chose a stuffed brown elephant with a bright red blanket on its back. She promptly named the new elephant Romeo "because," she explained, "every Juliette must have a Romeo."[6]

The vivacious and creative Juliette never found her Romeo during her brief lifetime of thirty-six years. In the summer of 1897, Minna's first two letters were addressed to her beloved younger sister, the most feminine of sisters who longed to be a soldier boy.

Letters from the front, summer of 1897

>Midland Hotel,
>Kansas City, Mo.
>No. 1 to Juliette,
>June 3, 1897

You needn't flatter yourself that I am using valuable time writing letters, we must wait here for two hours and I have to amuse myself somehow. They told us in N.Y. that we would have to wait in Chicago on Wednesday, when the California Limited (Santa Fe R.R.) leaves at six o'clock. I can tell you that we were pretty thankful, for it was raining household pets (don't you think that a more elegant expression than "cats and dogs"?) and the prospect of waiting eight hours in the subdued and dismal ladies' waiting room of Dearborn Station was not altogether cheering. I am grateful to that same waiting room, however, for three hours spent in a *rocking chair* (think of it!) reading *Harper's Magazine*. That part was not half bad, neither was the lunch we had in the station, though there could not have been a cubic inch of fresh air in the whole restaurant.

Alas for our beautiful plans of making calls on friends and 155 State St. near Monroe![7] They all vanished in mist. (Poetic for a good, hard rain.)

Tell Nan that her flowers have kept remarkably well, and my sweet peas are as fresh as when she gave them to me. They are a joy forever, though we don't see them much of the time, for we are saving them to wear at the fort. On each new train the porter takes charge of them for us, and when we leave gives them back in such a dripping state that we wish we had brought our mackintoshes.

The royal progress of the Misses Hollenback, a telescope, a dress-suit case, two bags, a camera, a box of candy, ditto of lunch, two magazines, two umbrellas, four large bunches of flowers and a porter is as well worth seeing as a procession, and I wonder that the crowds do not pause in astonishment as we go by. By the way, that despised lunch, spurned by the haughty officials of the Black Diamond, has been our salvation, though it was my own fault that we needed saving. The morning after we left Buffalo, "Miss Minna," who, you know, is "one of the easy-going ones," took a little too much of her own time and was pulled away from the dressing room to say good-bye to the dining car, which was leaving us with our expected breakfast, on board. So we fell back joyfully on hard-boiled eggs and dry sandwiches, (bless Nan for putting butter in them!) and sent the porter for milk at the next station.

If there is anything erratic and frivolous in this letter, and I doubt if there is much else, —blame our last waiter. He insisted on making a punkah-wallah of himself, and fanning us with a slow and stately motion worthy of an Egyptian slave.[8] Result, —I disgraced myself for the first time this trip by a giggling fit that shook gloves and packages onto the floor and lasted as long as that solemn breeze kept on. The well-meaning but undeserving Josephine kept making mildly funny remarks to cover my retreat and hers, till I was afraid that I couldn't stop in time to take the Leavenworth train.

I must cease from troubling, as we must go to the station in time to collect our impedimenta, which were left in charge of the Tenth Legion, otherwise the parcel room.

[Postscript] We are well, sleep beautifully and have alarming appetites. Mrs. Stevens won't want to keep us long. . . .[9]

Fort Leavenworth, Kansas
June 4, 1897

My dear General [Juliette],

There are three other people whom I should bother a little before writing to you again, but I only have your kind of things to say, so here goes.

Seems to me we have been here a month, that the whole family knows all about it and there is no need to tell them anything. Why don't we live in an army post? I wish you were a boy going to West Point. Privately, I think that there is no place on earth so beautiful as the Wyoming Valley [Pa.], but any unprejudiced critic ought to say that if there is anywhere in America an ideal spot for a home, this is it. It has the reputation of being the most beautiful post in the country, not even excepting West Point, though the Hudson gives a more beautiful water view than the Missouri. It is, I think, the largest, as it is one of the oldest of our army posts, and has by far the finest parade, although West Point approaches it.[10] Everything here seems to be the "most" something. I tell you all this so that you may see what advantages these untutored Eastern girls are enjoying, and repent of your error in staying in so hopelessly "civil" a place as 460 Washington Avenue in Brooklyn.

The country around here is a little bit English in character, though it is a little freer and not so prim and cotton-woolly. Soft round hills roll away in every direction, those that have not been cleared covered with thick forest. There is an air of rich abundance in the very shape of the trees, which are full-branched and symmetrical, prosperous forest citizens, not warped and twisted in the fight with unfriendly elements that stunts our Glen Summit trees into such sturdy angles.

The reservation is quite large, with hills and woods and farms and a cemetery. Mrs. Stevens's house is part of an old condemned barrack, which is being used for student officers' quarters until the authorities see fit to tear it down. But it faces on the main parade, and outside of an English park you never saw anything lovelier than that. Didn't you think that a parade was a flat square of bare sand with a row of houses all alike, on one side and some barracks on the other? This one is a big undulating lawn, most carefully kept, and spotted with great shady trees. They don't have cavalry parades on it, those are held on the west parade, which is larger, treeless except on the edges, and where the grass is not quite so fine. There is a full regiment of infantry here, the 20th, and I can tell you they march like clockwork; it looks as if done by electricity. Their colonel is in command of the post, their lieut. Col. is also here and a cavalry col. has something to do with the school. Pretty well supplied, isn't it? Four troops of the Sixth Cavalry are stationed here, four more at Fort Myer and the other two in the Yellowstone [Wyo.].[11]

The night we came there was a regimental dress parade right in front of the house, and next night a review of the whole garrison by the K.O. [commanding officer] on the west parade. We are in luck to have come at just this time of the week. I wanted to shout at retreat that first night. Directly in front of us the whole 20th regiment was stretched in a double line clear across the parade, commissioned officers in a line in front and non-coms behind; parade front, I think they call it.

The band was at the end of the line nearest us. As the sun went down, the evening gun was fired, the garrison flag was hauled down, the band played the "Star Spangled Banner" and all the officers not on parade took off their hats. Parade or not, the "S.S.B." is always played at retreat, except Sundays. After that the trumpeters blew the retreat. By the way, that is used at sundown and has nothing to do with retreating in battle. For that they sound the recall, pronounced re´-call, not re-call´.

People here always take off their hats to the flag. I wonder why citizens don't do so? And did you know that officers don't salute each other except on duty? When they pass in the street they raise their hats, like other people, but if a soldier passes an officer, he salutes and the officer does too. I have learned some things, but if I misinform you, don't blame me too much, for I have asked so many senseless questions that I know everyone is tired of it, and now I humbly take what I can get.

Mr. Stevens's regiment, the Ninth Cavalry, is not stationed here. He is one of the officers who are here on a special detail to take a course in the post-graduate school. The present class are taking their final exams. After graduating they leave here and others take their places.[12] It must seem hard, after only two years in this place of green trees, to go back to a barren frontier post.

An army post is near to every corner of the earth, at least you would suppose so from the nonchalant way in which the people speak of going almost anywhere. They are all equally familiar with Arizona and old Mexico or N.Y. and Brooklyn streets, and it must seem to them a little thing for their Eastern friends to demur at a comfortable railroad journey, when they themselves take it as a matter of course if they can only reach the nearest railway station by a four days' ambulance ride over roads so rough as to make some people seasick. There is a Mrs. Stanton here who was probably the first white woman to see the Grand Cañon and the Snake Dance, and who was also the first woman except the discoverer's wife to see some important Egyptian discovery, —I think it was a small temple. She has been nearly everywhere.[13]

Flagstaff, June 10.

This has been lying around in my bag til it has grown to be a good old age, but you might as well have it. There was so much to do in Ft. L. that we wouldn't have had time to admire the parade, if we couldn't have watched it and talked to people at the same time. By parade I mean the parade ground.

Mrs. Stevens's friends must have used most of their spare time in making us enjoy ourselves. I wish I had counted the number of callers, for I didn't keep any of their cards except those of Col. Hawkins, who is the K.O., and Mrs. Hawkins.[14]

We have been on three most beautiful drives. Once Col. and Mrs. Chaffee took us through Sheridan's Drive and turned off on a road prominently marked "Danger" on account of the rifle ranges near by. They supposed that there was no target practice that day, but they were mistaken, and it was mildly exciting to hear the cracking and banging and know that a curious bullet might try to find out what we were doing there.[15]

But the greatest excitement was when the doctor [Maj. Henry McElderry, fort physician] took us to the Soldiers' Home in a dog-cart. Mrs. Stevens and I sat on the back seat, and the doctor likes to go. So does his horse. At first I tried to keep my dignity and my hands in my lap, thinking it might be good practice in case I might want to enlist in the artillery. But that cart was too much for me. In a little while I was glad enough to hold on and vainly wish for a handle for the other hand. Once I bounced clear off the seat at the same time that my feet flew off the foot rest, but inertia, or something, brought me down in the right place.

That Soldiers' Home is a wonder, especially the kitchen and mess hall.[16] The kitchen is a place that would delight Annie's heart if she saw the immense quantities of things cooked there. And clean! One of the things to do is to wipe out the garbage tank with your handkerchief and see if you can find a speck of dust there. Jo did it, and used the handkerchief afterwards. The windows are open and without screens, and after careful search I discovered *one* lonely fly. A sight of the big shiny coffee kettles would make you decide to live there, and the bushels of carefully scrubbed potatoes going into one of the steam ovens to be baked almost did the same for me.

The work is all done by the soldiers, who take turns and are paid extra for it. There is an old sergeant at the head of the cooking department, and you ought to see what a beautiful system is kept up. At one end of the mess hall is a refrigerator composed of an ice chamber and a lot of little shallow drawers with wire bottoms. In each drawer is a certain number of butter plates with little pats of butter all ready for use, and on a table near by are piles and piles of plates of ready-cut bread, very nice looking bread it is, too.

There were dishes of apple sauce, or something, set in rows on big open shelves, which run on wheels. These shelves are run right up to the dining tables, and it is easy to see that such things might be done very quickly, but how quickly is beyond guessing. At twelve o'clock 1,080 men sit down to dinner, and at 12:30 the dishes have been washed and the table set for the next installment. And they do not have small dinners.

Much to my sorrow, I got hardly any pictures of Leavenworth. There were so many calls to be returned, and that inconsiderate old sun kept going just far enough behind the clouds to keep me from taking snap shots, which were my only dependence as I had foolishly left my tripod in the other trunk. I did take guard-mounting one morning hoping to get something recognizable, although the light was too dim for a good picture.

Jo was inconsolable the day we left, because there would be no gun and bugles to wake her up next morning. I offered to buy a tin horn and blow reveille for her every day, but even that didn't cheer her up a bit. We are both decided that Flagstaff is not quite all it should be, for there is no fort here. You can't think how we miss those same old tootings. It is so easy to think you hear them, and then wake up and find you don't. I have to whistle taps every night to put myself to sleep. Oh, to always have my trunk carried around in a wagon marked "U.S.," and always drive to the station in a jolting old ambulance drawn by four of what Dr. McEldery [sic] calls "the quartermasters mewels"!

Mrs. Stevens gave a card party for us Saturday night. Only the student officers and their wives were invited, and my dear, those men came in *dress suits!* If they knew how much more distinguished they look in any sort of a uniform, they wouldn't reduce themselves to such an ordinary-looking assemblage, for their dress suits didn't all fit well, and that's one thing that can't be said of a uniform. You see, the proper thing to wear in the evening is a full-dress uniform, but those were so heavy and padded as to be very hot indoors. And I suppose they like to wear something different at parties from what they wear at school, so most of them put on dress suits, though many keep on their uniforms and look comfortable.

Jo lost her camera while looking for maidenhair ferns. It dropped from her wheel [bicycle] without her noticing it; and although she could probably have found it, she had no time to go back. They didn't want her to go alone, anyhow, for fear she might meet a prisoner who could get away on her wheel. There is a large prison on the post. It was formerly a military prison, but has been turned over to the federal authorities.[17]

Some exciting stories are told of attempted escapes by the prisoners from the guard-house. These (soldiers, *not* convicts from the prison) cut the grass and do other work about the post, with a sentinel in charge of every one or two prisoners. Once, when two prisoners were working by a ditch, at the same instant one seized their sentinel's gun while the other one held the sentinel, then they pitched him over the bank. But the man held his gun so tight that the prisoner who had grabbed it was jerked over after him, and they both rolled down together. Then there was a scuffle, but the sentinel finally regained his gun, and making no attempt to shoot, marched them both back to the guard house, which people here seem to think was showing a good deal of self-control for a recruit. But after all that, that man was *scared*. He was afraid of being killed if he stayed in the same regiment with those men. So after getting permission to carry a pistol, and after vainly trying to have himself exchanged to another post, he quietly deserted, took the first train to Fort Riley and gave himself up for arrest. He had no intention of deserting, but was ready to do anything to get away from that post. The charge brought against him was "absence without leave."

I have a grudge against Fort Riley.[18] For a year past the Leavenworth people have been trying to get up different games between the two posts. Last fall the Riley football team was to come here, but there was some hitch and they didn't appear. Last Saturday was to be the day of a great baseball game. The two teams had been practising for some time, the Riley team and a lot of Riley men had come 150 miles to Leavenworth, officers and men, women and children, had carried their chairs on to the west parade, the Leavenworth team was on the ground, when word came that the Rileys wouldn't play. Why? Because their new uniforms hadn't come! Of all reasons for men who are supposed to mean business! And the light was just right for a snap shot. When you understand that it was not a matter of postponing the game, but of giving it up altogether, you will see that such an excuse would seem just a little bit silly.

I find that I have been calling Leavenworth "here." It is no wonder, for I am just the opposite of that soldier who tried so hard to get away; I would do almost anything to get back there.

If you are completely exhausted by this long piece of stupidity, take a rest and don't read the next one. It won't hurt you, now that school is over. . . .

Jo is writing a regular book of travel to send Papa. She calls it a letter. . . . It was her pocket Kodak that Jo lost. She misses it dreadfully & her films are now useless. Why don't you send her a new one![19]

On June 1, 1897, the day Minna and Jo left New York on the first leg of their trip west, a rare summer snow squall swept over the Hudson River, creating the light and cloud effect Minna described in her diary. That same day an earthquake was felt from western Pennsylvania into North Carolina and Tennessee. Another coincidence also marked the Hollenback sisters' train ride from Fort Leavenworth to Flagstaff. An army of 15,000 tramps on freight trains was also working its way west. They were following the path of 55,000 tourists belonging to the Young People's Society of the Christian Endeavor, who were en route to their national convention in San Francisco—a lucrative source for panhandlers.[20]

By traveling to the American Southwest in 1897, Minna and Jo Hollenback showed the love of adventure for which they were well known among their peers. Far from the sitting room of their Brooklyn residence, they would discover the western woman's unbridled sense of place and self in a cultural world strange to their Pennsylvania and New York heritage but still within their country.

The girls' letters reveal the insecurities and inconveniences of single Victorian women traveling in the Southwest, as well as their first impressions of westerners and the Pueblo Indian culture and their earnest concern for future Southwest archaeological conservation. Of historical significance, photographs taken in Arizona and New Mexico Territories in 1897 by amateur Amelia Hollenback are some of the earliest by a woman tourist in the area presently known.

The Southwest adventure of the Hollenback sisters began at a time when religion could still dominate the news of the day in the eastern United States. A plea for Puritanism echoed from the baccalaureate sermon that year at Amherst College in Massachusetts,[21] but meanwhile out west, a small railroad town called Flagstaff flaunted its unpuritanical ways.

Notes

1. Mrs. JWH to husband, Nov. 14 and Dec. 17, 1897, HC.

2. The Black Diamond Express, the fastest train of the Lehigh Valley Railroad, began its run in 1896 and traveled from New York to Buffalo in ten hours; it burned anthracite, called "black diamond," in its steam engine. The black-painted station platform symbolized the train's route through northeastern Pennsylvania and its coalfields. The train made its last run on May 11, 1959. Harwood, "Corporate History of the Lehigh Valley R.R." Charlotte Corday stabbed to death Jean-Paul Marat during the French Revolution, an act for which she was imprisoned, then guillotined in 1793.

3. ABH Expense diary, HC. Mrs. Stevens was the wife of Lt. Charles Josiah Stevens of the Ninth Cavalry, who left Fort Leavenworth soon after the visit of the Hollenback sisters. Heitman, *Historical Register and Dictionary*, 1:922.

4. The Hollenbacks were among the first to perceive that the chief commodity of railroads would be coal. Blacksmiths in Wilkes-Barre, Pa., had burned anthracite as early as 1769, obtaining it from the Hollenback Mill Creek Mine by 1776, six years after Matthias Hollenback (Minna and Jo's maternal grandfather) arrived in Wyoming Valley. In 1807 scholar Jacob Cist married the daughter of Matthias, who controlled 48,500 acres of coal land, making Hollenback one of the earliest anthracite land barons. Anthracite's durability, longevity, and even heat made it valuable; it was also cleaner to burn, a fact early recognized by Cist. Scientists, financiers, and politicians all greatly respected Jacob Cist's knowledge of Pennsylvania's anthracite formation, and his notes and drawings remain the earliest and

most accurate. Cist died in 1825 at age forty-three, before the beginning of the Industrial Revolution in the U.S., spawned by the coal he sought to commercialize. Sarsfield, "Matthias Hollenback," 22, 59, 61, 88; Powell, *Philadelphia's First Fuel Crisis*, 15-16, 55.

5. Durham boats were approximately 40 ft. long with an 8 ft. beam, poled along by four men, two on each side, who walked along the running boards. Myers and Hanlon, *Historical Album of Wilkes-Barre and Wyoming Valley*, 38.

6. The story of Romeo the elephant was told to the author in 1983 by Elizabeth Twyeffort Drake, daughter-in-law of Josephine Hollenback Twyeffort.

7. This was the address in Chicago of the Huyler chocolate factory.

8. A *punkah* is a fan made from the palmyra leaf; *punkah-wallah* was the name given to an Indian servant who fans the air with a punkah.

9. ABH to Juliette, June 3, 1897, HC.

10. Fort Leavenworth, Kans., near present-day Kansas City, Mo., was established by Col. Henry Leavenworth in 1827 as the first fort west of the Missouri River. Then officially called Cantonment Leavenworth, the fort's primary mission from 1830-1870 was to protect wagon trains headed west along the Santa Fe and Oregon Trails against Indian attacks. By 1881 Fort Leavenworth had become the U.S. Army Command and General Staff College to train officers in advanced military thought and methods of warfare. Today the fort is a modern military post and the headquarters of the Combined Arms Center of the Army, which trains qualified officers of the National Guard and Organized Reserves for leadership; it is registered as a national historic site. Hunt, *History of Fort Leavenworth*, 17–18, 26–27, 136, 203.

11. The Stevenses lived in dilapidated barracks constructed in the 1830s for the First Regiment of Dragoons, which became the First Regiment of the U.S. Cavalry. By 1897 families of students at Fort Leavenworth were living in these old quarters that stood on the east side of Main Parade. The barracks were torn down in 1903, and the site is now a grassy, open area across from the Memorial Chapel. Hunt, *History*, 52; Langellier to author, July 25, 1984. Fort Myer, Va., founded in 1863 on the southern bank of the Potomac, became one of the principal defenses of Washington during the Civil War; first called Fort Whipple, its name was changed to Fort Myer in 1881. Prucha, *Guide to the Military Posts*, 93.

12. In June 1897 the troops at Fort Leavenworth consisted of four troops of the Sixth Cavalry, ten companies of the Twentieth Infantry, Lieutenant Stevens from the Ninth Cavalry, and another person from the Seventeenth Infantry. Stevens, along with many others, was relieved of duty during June. Within a short time the Spanish-American War of 1898, plus the Philippine Insurrection, caused a four-year suspension of the army's systematic education program. Hunt, *History*, 50; Jochims to author, Aug. 27, 1982.

13. An ambulance wagon generally conveyed the sick or wounded; however, in the nineteenth-century West, the term also applied to wagons used as traveling carriages. Amelia may have referred to the wife of William Stanton, son of General Henry Stanton and grandson of General Alexander Macomb, who commanded the army from 1835-1841. Altshuler File, FVA. Although it is not known which white woman first saw Grand Canyon, Mrs. Edward E. Ayer is credited with being the first to descend to the bottom. Barnes, *Arizona Place Names*, 1937; *Arizona Champion*, May 23, 1885. To date no documentation has been found of the first non-Indian woman to witness a Hopi Snake Dance, although Albuquerque photographer W. Calvin Brown, who photographed the Walpi dance in 1885, noted that spectators there included two ladies from Navajo Springs. *Albuquerque Weekly Journal*, Aug. 24, 1885. The Mrs. Stanton-

Egyptian reference could not be found.

14. "K.O.," rather than "C.O.," was used when referring to the commanding officer's wife to avoid the abbreviation of "C.O.W." While at Fort Leavenworth, Minna and Jo hobnobbed with some of the best-known nineteenth-century soldiers in America. Col. Hamilton S. Hawkins of the Twentieth Cavalry was commandant of the command and general staff school in Fort Leavenworth between Oct. 1894 and April 1898; he achieved prominence during the Spanish-American War before retiring in Oct. 1898. Heitman, *Register*, 513; Hunt, *History*, 224.

15. In June 1897 Col. Adna Romanza Chaffee was in charge of the Dept. of Cavalry at Fort Leavenworth; he distinguished himself as a "determined" but "humane" soldier between 1861 and 1906, fighting in fifty battles from the Civil War to the Boxer Rebellion in China. While stationed at Fort Verde in 1882, he gained fame at the Battle of Big Dry Wash during the Apache Indian uprisings led by Geronimo, Victorio, Cochise, and Mangas Coloradas. (The name Big Dry Wash was the one adopted for East Clear Creek in the official report.) Chaffee was captain of the Gray Horse Troop of the Sixth Cavalry. In 1906 he retired to Los Angeles where he served as the first president of the Southwest Museum founded by Charles F. Lummis. His friend and admirer, Lummis once challenged Chaffee to a swearing contest for a museum benefit, commenting, "He [Chaffee] had the advantage in Reach and Volume but he could only swear in English; whereas I could throw in several more in Spanish with minor furbelows in French, German and a few Indian tunes. . . ." Chaffee, the "grim old warrior" known for his profane language during battle, confided that he had sworn off swearing, with the confession that "I have become a Christian Scientist." *Dictionary of American Biography*, 3:589; Carter, *Life of Chaffee*, 96–97, 121–22, 277–86; Fiske and Lummis, *Charles F. Lummis*, 146.

16. A branch of the National Home for Disabled Volunteer Soldiers (known as Wadsworth and the forerunner of the V.A. Medical Center) was founded in Fort Leavenworth in 1885. Leavenworth County Museum, brochure.

17. In 1875 a military prison was established at Fort Leavenworth; it was used as a civil prison from 1895 to 1906, when it again became a military prison. The name was changed in 1915 from the United States Military Prison to the United States Disciplinary Barracks, and in 1929 the barracks were turned over to the Department of Justice. The United States Penitentiary, established in 1896 on part of the reservation, is a civil prison with little or no contact with the military there, although the law of establishment states that "this prison reservation shall be open for military tactical purposes, when such purposes do not interfere with the discipline of said prison." Hunt, *History*, 208–13.

18. Fort Riley, Kansas, was originally established in 1853 with the name of Camp Center because of its geographical location in the United States, near Junction City. Prucha, *Guide*, 102; Grant, *American Forts*, 243; Frazer, *Forts of the West*, 57.

19. ABH to Juliette, June 4 to 10, 1897.

20. *New York Times*, June 1, 26, and 29, 1897; *Los Angeles Daily Times*, July 30, 1897. Christian Endeavor Societies, interdenominational and international, were founded in 1881 by Dr. Francis E. Clark of Portland, Maine, for the purpose of promoting spiritual life among young people. Apparently, the societies conveniently served as marriage brokers as well.

21. *New York Times*, June 28, 1897.

CHAPTER TWO

There's Nothing Puritanical about Flagstaff

FLAGSTAFF, ARIZONA TERRITORY, advertised itself in 1897 as the "Skylight City, Gateway to Grand Canyon, and unpuritanical."[1] Of equal importance to the town's economy was the railroad track that paralleled the south side of Flagstaff's one-sided main street, apparently known by two names, Railroad Avenue and Front Street. For well over a decade before 1897, Flagstaffians had witnessed the arrival and departure of Atlantic & Pacific trains linking the East with the West.

The abundant forests and nearby sawmills of Flagstaff furnished the Atlantic & Pacific Railroad ties for many miles. Over these ties the first official through-passenger service from Albuquerque, New Mexico, to San Francisco, California, began in August 1883. Within four years, a man named Fred Harvey was serving hot meals to hungry passengers in the Arizona towns of Williams and Winslow. Flagstaff, though bypassed by Harvey's depot restaurants, was already courting its destiny—lumber, cattle, sheep, and tourists. Destiny, nevertheless, would rearrange the order of business when, soon after the turn of the twentieth century, both tourists and Fred Harvey discovered the awesome chasm to the north called Grand Canyon.

Before Fred Harvey opened the log-cabin hotel El Tovar, on Grand Canyon's South Rim in 1905, single women traveling to the canyon depended on local contacts for information. Staunch Presbyterians, Minna and Jo Hollenback had inquired at the Fifth Avenue Presbyterian Church in New York City about the Rev. Harry Prosper Corser of Flagstaff. He measured up to their high standards for masculine company, with the added plus of being a bachelor. A recent graduate of Union Theological Seminary in New York City, the newly appointed Reverend Corser offered to introduce the sisters to influential members of his Flagstaff congregation and to accompany them on some of their outings, properly chaperoned by his women parishioners. By summer's end, the Reverend Corser's clapboard church would enjoy a fresh coat of paint with the help of a Hollenback contribution. The Presbyterians were quick to welcome "A. B. And C. J. [J. W.] Hollenback," as they were called by the local newspaper, the

Flagstaff Sun-Democrat. Minna later commented on the fact that women in the West lacked given names.[2]

By the time the sisters arrived in Flagstaff, all of northern Arizona firmly believed there was no uncertainty about the town's future. It was everywhere, quite literally in the air. Flagstaff's air and its unexcelled atmospheric qualities were recognized as early as 1894 by Harvard astronomers Percival Lowell and Andrew Endicott Douglass, when they established Lowell Observatory in order to view Mars and its canals. Then a Flagstaff winter set in, and snowy clouds blanketed the San Francisco Peaks nearby, obscuring all visibility of outer space for the stargazers.

Lowell wrote that the seeing was perpetually poor. Consequently, in 1895 an alternate location near Mexico City was chosen, and the Flagstaff observatory almost dismantled. By early 1897 atmospheric conditions encouraged a return to the Flagstaff site despite the northern Arizona winters, and the dome used in Mexico was erected on Mars Hill west of Railroad Avenue. Triumphantly, the *Flagstaff Sun-Democrat* announced, "Skylight City Beats Mexico," with all the enthusiasm of an Olympic victory.[3]

Perhaps it was the advertisements for Flagstaff as being "highly impregnated with ozone air, almost to the point of intoxication" that caused Minna and Jo to be so attracted to the town and its unpretentious people. Whatever the reason, the sisters found it filled with folk who steadfastly believed in the potential of their piney area and valued the historic significance of the surrounding cliff dwellings and canyons.

Like many other Americans in the late nineteenth century, the Hollenback sisters believed the cliff dwellings were about to be destroyed (and some were) and that the surviving Indian culture of the Southwest itself stood on the brink of extinction. In 1898, only a year after their visit, a smallpox epidemic devastated Zuni Pueblo, and many Hopi Indians also died. Minna particularly felt an urgency to sound the alarm for Indian cultural preservation, a pursuit she followed the rest of her long life. Conservation of Arizona's historic sites came none too soon. Visitors today, unlike Minna and Jo in 1897, cannot slide down the volcanic-cinder mountain called Sunset Crater or climb ladders to the top of the Verde Valley cliff dwelling known as Montezuma Castle.

Frontier Arizona had awakened to its outstanding anthropological legacy by the year 1897, which saw significant changes in the economy of the Southwest as well. Construction of the Santa Fe & Grand Canyon Railroad from Williams to Grand Canyon began (completed in 1901), and the Atlantic & Pacific Railroad was absorbed by the Santa Fe Railway. With the help of Fred Harvey, the Santa Fe would put Arizona's Grand Canyon on the map through colorful tourists brochures. Despite these economic changes that would so much affect the region's future, Minna and Jo found northern Arizona still a land of ancient mystery. To them it became a place where the soul knew no boundaries and where the spirit might remain suspended over the untamed landscape as if in an immortal summer.

The research Minna had done at the Smithsonian two months earlier—and the lectures she attended in Brooklyn—had primed her for the first actual encounters with native cultures in the Southwest. It is clear from the following letters she wrote home that this was not a spur-of-the-moment trip but one that fulfilled a "dream of many years," and that she was seeing her "dearest hopes so realized." From these we can see how deeply and passionately she responded to this new world. The roots of her attraction to the peoples and architecture of the region were firmly planted, leading eventually to her collaboration with John Gaw Meem to build her Santa Fe home in 1932.

Before leaving for Grand Canyon, both girls wrote to their parents; Minna sent the following to her mother.

New Bank Hotel,
Flagstaff, Arizona
June 13, 1897

If you ever had any lingering visions of your two children trying to keep up each other's courage during a long tropic day, you may banish them right away. This air is like Glen Summit water, cool, refreshing as if its own sunshine lived in one's every fiber, and a blessing to dust-weary railroad travellers. The first thing that struck me was that this was exactly the climate that you would enjoy, yet they say this is the most disagreeable month of summer! The air is dry enough to delight a lecturer on static electricity; when I comb my hair it stands out like so many wires. Flagstaff is built on a great piney highland that cuts into the desert around the San Francisco mountains, and you wouldn't believe, to see it, that there could be a desert in the same country. But this is nothing but an island.

Think of me with awe, for I have seen some cliff-dwellings! I started this letter a day or two ago and I don't remember what I intended to tell you, but whatever it was, it must wait. For yesterday was one of my big red-letter days and I can think of nothing else. Was I happy scrambling around that cañon [Walnut Canyon], poking into those funny little houses, getting dusty and scratched up and forgetting everything else in the world but Glen Summit?[4] I wonder.

Mrs. Sisson (I don't know how she spells her name) whose husband is treasurer of the big lumber company here, invited two ladies and ourselves to drive out to the cliffs with her, and my, but it was fun!⁵ We started off in a three-seated ambulance (the eternal fitness of things couldn't have been heard of when that wagon was named), and a [few] miles from town it calmly began to rain. They don't stop for thunder, lightning or volcanic eruptions in this country, so when the rain turned into a good hard hailstorm we let down the curtains and went cheerfully on. Maybe a combination of rain, hail and thunder is not your idea of the "land of sunshine," but I have no fault to find with that name. This is the first time in many years that there has been any rain here before July; it is an old tradition that the first rain comes on the Fourth. In the rainy season there is a shower every day, sometimes hard and fierce, sometimes not enough to lay the dust, but the showers are short and small in extent, with plenty of sunshine sprinkled in between. So we expected to leave the shower behind us before long, and sure enough, the cañon was as dry as if water was a thing unknown, although there was a little stream at the bottom. There is one queer thing about these cañons. You can get almost within a few yards of one without knowing it is there, so level is this planed-off country, and so suddenly do the great walls fall away from the plains around them. I suppose I had no business to be so impressed with a little cañon scarcely taller than three large pine trees, but when we had taken a few steps through the forest and that wide awful crack opened before our eyes, I declare it seemed as it nothing less majestic than a thunderstorm ought ever to darken those bare walls with its shadow.

In my memory the cañon wears a friendly, even a welcoming air, for I have clambered down its sides and been within the walls that once made homes along its ledges, but at first sight it held me off as if an invisible presence had said "Thus far, and no farther," and I actually shook when we started down the rocks, as if we had no right to be there. Mrs. Sisson laughed when I said it looked immense, but perhaps years of think[ing] and longing magnified that first reality. A dream come true must always be a little startling.

That scribble is not supposed to look like the cañon. I was going to cut it out but Jo said to leave it in and say that Romeo's ladder climbing up hill is a river. The cliff-dwellings [in the drawing] are too large and too perfect and on the wrong side of the cañon excepting one. Also there should be trees in the bottom.

There is one reason why the people of these United States should be ashamed of themselves, and that is because of their neglect, and worse, of memorials such as this world will never see again. For progress cannot be stopped, our descendants will see flying machines and wonders we never dreamed of, but who can call back one day of the forgotten times whose story we can but guess? In the old country, workers have for many years been trying to wring a meager knowledge of our far-off ancestors from the few accidental relics that time has left us there, but here are hundreds living a chapter of life that other people have long passed by or else will never know. I suppose the African tribes will have no time to work themselves naturally into the stage of advancement where the Pueblos are now; civilization is crowding them so closely that they must jump straight from savagery to our modern customs. Here, by our very sides, are passing the lost remnants of that closing chapter; strange old cities that defied the fierce Apache are falling before the carelessness of the modern relic hunters; habits and religions older than they are fading from the land where they ruled so long.

What object lessons are here for young or old who would know something of how their ancestors fought and toiled to reach the level where we stand today, or something of scenes and peoples as strangely remote from ourselves and far more interesting than any of the mythical races with which the imaginative Europeans once filled all central Asia. Better than the dead pages of any history or story book, only a few miles from the railroad are the living realities of which we read with such wonder, and the stern old piles that held them safely in days when life was not so secure as now.

Oh, if parents who are able to travel would only realize that this is a needed part of education that no school can supply, and bring their older children here that they may have it indelibly graven on their minds, as only seeing can engrave it! Those fortunate young people would have a store of better than fairy tales to tell their own children more vividly than pen could ever picture them, for not many generations will have the opportunities that some of this day are throwing away. Tenacious though they may be of their old customs, the Pueblos cannot long hold to the queer habits and ceremonials which are disappearing even now. Their very traditions would soon be lost forever, as any knowledge depending on the verbal transmission of solemn beliefs must be lost when the beliefs die out and books come in, were it not for the labors of a few determined scientists, much fewer than we could wish them to be.

As for the care which is usually given to old ruins, I will give you an example. "Montezuma's Castle," which they say is the noblest, though not the largest, of the more imposing cliff cities, is being so undermined by relic-hunters that its walls are in immediate danger of falling. Not by scientific expeditions, mind you, but by ignorant travellers. A short while ago some intelligent Arizonians sent a petition to their legislature asking for some protection of this priceless monument. And what was their answer? "Oh, let them knock it down, if they want to; it brings people here." Queer policy, wasn't it? As if people in the near future would come to see the pile of stones that the satisfied relic-hunters left! Think of the coming students who may have to depend on a few photographs and writings, when they might have had the objects themselves to study if the present generation had been a little more thoughtful. A nice page it will make in our history if we oblige our chroniclers to state that the most inventive and progressive, and one of the most enlightened nations of the nineteenth century took no more care for its future education than that!

But Montezuma's Castle may be saved, for a young man in Flagstaff collected $500 and the former petitioners are now doing what they can by themselves. Let us hope that this awakening may be soon and strong enough to preserve the homes, though it cannot the surviving customs, of the ancient Pueblos.[6]

I find that I have been writing a kind of dissertation instead of a letter. Of course, all this indignant information is copied, and you have heard it many times before. But it comes with such new force to a person here so near what seems the exit of bygone ages, that I had to say it to someone, and you are so patient with my talking attacks that I hope you will forgive it.

Isn't it lovely, the way people are planning our trips for us and taking care of us generally? It is nearly all due to Mr. Corser, for almost everyone we have met has said that Mr. Corser told them we were coming and they hadn't called yet because they didn't know that we had already arrived. It is a great thing to be able to take our longest trip, that to the Natural Bridge and Montezuma's Well and Castle, with friends, instead of being obliged to accept the company of anyone who might want to go in that direction, or else stay home.[7]

You needn't be afraid, however, that we may have to take what we can get, for every summer parties of residents go on the different trips we want to take, and they are so hospitable to visitors that they are sure to ask us to go with them. If they didn't, we should only have to wait till a congenial party started from the hotel, for a little later in the season this is a great place for professors' families and other intelligent travellers. (Ahem!) The professional globe-trotters haven't found out this place as thoroughly as they will later, but the array of celebrities who have been here is fairly dazzling, and sometimes they have regular Brooklyn Institute courses of lectures by their summer visitors. Jo and I may join the list later, but we are preparing to modestly decline any invitations to address audiences of professors here this summer.[8]

It is comforting not to feel alone, but do you know, it is awfully disappointing not to have a chance of exercising that American independence we were so proud of. Everything goes with as discouraging smoothness as it would at home, and you would think the woolly West was hopelessly tame. We don't even have to cash our own checks; the proprietor [of the New Bank Hotel], Mr. Tolfree, obligingly takes them out and cashes them for us. And we won't have to use any rope ladders to get to the bottom of the Cañon, for there are three trails by which one can ride horseback to the river itself.[9]

We are going to the Cañon to-morrow (Monday) and please don't expect me to say anything about it, for it would take more cheek than I possess to make one try to describe the grandest sight on earth. I only hope we will have strength of mind enough to come back as soon as we ought, for there is nothing that would make us want to leave that place. No, I am wrong, there is one thing, which I will speak of later.

They say that we will have no climbing in the Cañon, as hard as that we did at the cliffs last Friday, though there are plenty of all-but-impossible climbs for those who want to take them. That news was a relief to us, as we had expected to leave some important things undone, but judging from the cliff trail, we can do everything that ordinary people who are not mountaineers usually accomplish. The cliff trail was very easy indeed for anyone not leading a storming party against one of those swallow's nests called cliff-dwellings. But I can't possibly see how Apaches, or any one else, ever took one of those fortresses, tiny though they are. The walls which are still standing seem thick and strong enough to resist anything but artillery or battering rams, and their prehistoric foes could not so much as hurl large stones against them, since each little house was so wedged in between ledges as to make that impossible. This is something like one of the Flagstaff cliff-dwellings when they were new. The upper ledge should overhang the lower one quite a good deal, and the house is supposed to be almost directly on the edge of the lower one. The little hole in front is a door. There were no windows. Below, as well as above, are the tiers and tiers of narrow, broken shelves, with their broad vertical faces of smooth-worn rock, and down this terrible staircase must they go, the people of the rocks, to fill their heavy water-jars at the little river and carry them back again to their eagle homes. Thus did the precious water protect itself and the people whose very existence depended upon it.

Now I want to consult you on a most important matter. Not about our health, for that was never better or had better prospect of remaining so. In plain English, we want to stay longer and do more than we at first expected to do. We want to go to the Snake Dance. I have to put it in simple statements, there are no words to tell how much we want it. It takes place every two years, in Hualpi (Wall´-pee) [Walpi] on the Moqui [Hopi] reservation. There is to be a big one this year, about the twelfth of August [actually Aug. 21]. It is always held at the time of the August full moon. Few white women have ever seen it, but a party from here will probably go this year. The journey is made by rail for a short distance [east to Canyon Diablo] then two or three days of wagon riding and camping. There is no danger, and no more discomfort than on the camping trips we are going to take.

That means practically none. People can stand on the roofs of houses if they like, or in other places nowhere near the snakes. In perhaps a few years it will have passed away with other ceremonies of its kind, and no one can see it then. There is no hesitation in our minds excepting on one point, and—as you must have guessed—that is money. Perhaps 150 extra apiece would more than do it; perhaps we should each need 200. The Hualpi trip would of course not cost that, but we should have about five weeks extra board to pay, and to economize time would be obliged to take an important side trip from here which we had expected to take on our way East. This would necessitate extra railroad fares. Also we will have to spend more on wagons and horses than we thought at first, although the board is lower than we had estimated.

In two or three weeks I shall probably be able to itemize more, but a long explanation would tell very little besides what I have already said. It seems a very cheeky thing to ask Papa to lend us three or four hundred more when he has already done so much. But you understand, don't you, that the reason we want to do this is the same that brought us here? Without exact data, it is hard to estimate the amount of money we shall need, but it seems to go a little faster than I had expected. Yet our only extravagance has been the purchase of three of Mr. Lummis's books because we were so pitiably ignorant about what we were going to see.[10]

Oh Mama, don't think our wanderings endless, and don't, don't mind refusing if you and Papa think best for us to come home at the first-appointed time. As for the length of this possible stay away from home, if you are willing and do not need Jo, there is no great objection to that. The Flagstaff climate is if anything better than Glen Summit; it is cooler in summer, and July and August are two of its pleasantest months, instead of the most uncomfortable, as they are with us. We could have no better place to recuperate if we needed it, as we don't and won't. It will not be so very long away from you all; and where fun is concerned, any amount of it would be a small equivalent for one of these camping trips. But don't think our happiness is in any way dependent on the particular trip I have mentioned; if no party goes from here it would be impossible anyway, though that is highly improbable. We had to know your opinion of it, as it might make some difference in our other plans.

When I think of Minna Hollenback standing in the places that the next three weeks will show us, it seems as if enough good fortune for half a lifetime had been poured out for that one person. Did anyone ever have so many of their dearest hopes so realized at one time, before? It seems as if my trees in Glen Summit must know I am here, and the rocks be glad because I am so happy. Perhaps this will reach you on your wedding day [anniversary]. How I wish I could hug you and Papa that once. May that day be as sunny for you as ours are, and always afterwards.[11]

Jo, the older and more sedate of the two sisters, wrote to their parents. Perhaps realizing that she lacked the exuberance and spontaneity of Minna in the storytelling department, she defers to her younger sister for further details.

June 13, 1897
. . .we have thought of you all up there [in Glen Summit] so many times, since the last letters came, and I only hope you are having as magnificent weather there as we are enjoying here. I was almost going to say "up there," when as a matter of fact we might look down on the dear old Summit from an altitude of nearly 5,000 feet above it, for we are here, to be exact, just 6,866 [6,894] feet above the sea, while San Francisco Mountains rise behind the town 6,000 feet more, the two highest peaks of which, always in summer have some snow at the summit, though not even now as much as I

expected to see. The climate here is perfectly delightful; it would make a fine summer resort, if the water supply was only adequate.

As Minna has probably told you, everyone here has been so kind to us. Mrs. Knox and her daughter, from Wisconsin, who are spending the summer here, on account of the latter's health, have made us feel so much at home. On our return from the Cañon we shall probably see a good deal more of them, as we shall make this, as we supposed, our headquarters and take different trips from here, and they may accompany us on one of them.

Miss Knox has been here two summers and is no longer an invalid, but is only staying longer to make the cure complete. . . .[12]

Mr. Corser it seems is *not* married, fortunately we discovered the fact through Mrs. Knox before we made any allusion to the mythical lady. As Mrs. Knox says he is "too much of an old bach" to make such a thing possible. He can't be much older than Ted Welles [a relative], but he certainly looks fifteen years his senior. I certainly understood at the Board rooms at first, that he was here "with his family," and I never thought to ask again.

Since our coming here, he has had another request for information in regard to the Grand Cañon, the Cliff-Dweller ruins, and other points of interest near, from a Dr. Kipp, so we are not the only ones "at sea."[13]

Mrs. Frederick Sisson, that friend of Mr. Corser's who took us to the Cliff-Dwellings, said she didn't see how we heard of Arizona, but we agree with her, that judging from what we know there is to be seen, that there can be no other spot on the globe which has more places of wonderful and mysterious interest, and scenic beauty within a radius of a hundred miles from it, than Flagstaff, Arizona; and out in this undeveloped country of magnificent distances a hundred miles seems more what twenty would at home.

If Mrs. Sisson gets up the party for the Natural Bridge, which she wants us to join when we get back from the Cañon, we will have a drive of eighty-five miles before we reach it. We hope on the same trip to visit Montezuma's Well and Castle. Mrs. Sisson's mother and father from the East are to visit her then, and she is anxious to have them both see those sights. We will be more fortunate if we can go with them and I think it is very kind of her to want us, as she has told Mr. Corser she does, for of course it will be the only way in which we could take such a long trip, for it will take us three days at the least; and the larger the party the smaller the expense for each. We like Mrs. Sisson so much. She is so ladylike and so bright and entertaining. She came here as a bride from the East, she said, ten years ago, and has been here ever since. Mrs. Knox says that her husband is as nice as she is. We haven't met him yet, as his business is at the lumber mills above Flagstaff, which keeps him there most of the time. . . .

Friday, after our return from the Cliff-Dwellings, Mrs. Knox introduced us at dinner to Prof. Douglas [sic], who is working at the Observatory here, and who almost immediately remarked that Mrs. Knox had told him that one of us had been to Mexico, and went on to say that he was at the Iturbide Hotel in the City of Mexico while we were there. The other members of our party may be interested to hear that he said further, that he and his fellow-business-exiles from home used to hang over the railings of the courtyard of the Iturbide, when any Raymond parties arrived, for they were "the only interesting looking Americans" they saw in the city! I wonder if that may be taken as a compliment or not, hardly so, I fear, if we were to be regarded in the light of a "circus," as some Raymond parties have been, we hear.[14]

It seems that there was some thought, last winter, of transferring most of the astronomical work done here to the City of Mexico, as that is about the same altitude. So that is why Prof. Douglas was there, but they found that the atmosphere is steadier here at Flagstaff. Prof. Lowell, who has done so much of his work on Mars from this observatory, is expected here again, they say, but at present Dr. Lea [T. J. J. See] whose speciality are the double stars, and Prof. Douglas, who works more with Jupiter, are both here. We haven't had the pleasure of meeting the first name gentleman as he sleeps all day, and works all night; but as Jupiter sets so early Prof. Douglas doesn't work so late; we came near meeting the first celebrity, however, last evening.[15]

Mr. Corser had asked permission to bring us up to the observatory, and both astronomers said they "would be pleased," etc., so we walked up last evening, one of the clearest moonlight nights we have either of us ever seen. The walk up the little mountain [Mars Hill] by the trail which is the shortest, took us about three-quarters of an hour, for we didn't hurry and stopped every once in a while to take in the magnificent beauty of the moonlit plain below. The want of underbrush here makes it possible to see through the forests for a great distance in every direction, and the moonlight falling through the tall straight pines made many weird as well as beautiful effects. The beauty of the San Francisco Peaks in the light, over to our left as we ascended, was beyond description. Almost every day since we came we have seen those mountains under a different aspect, they are always changing color, and the effect of sunlight and shadow, snow and cloud upon them make them a sight well worth a trip to see, but we are up so far ourselves, that it is hard to realize that they are nearly 13,000 [12,000] feet above sea level.

Well, last night we didn't have a peek at Jupiter, as we had hoped, for there was evidently some misunderstanding on Prof. Douglas's part, that he didn't expect us to go up last night, for that was one of the times when he didn't go himself, and although Dr. Lea [See] would have arrived about 9:30 p.m., we thought we had better not wait that late, so we started down a few minutes after nine.

We felt well repaid for the walk, however, by the beauty of the views both going up and coming down, and Mr. Corser says we will try it again when we return from the Cañon, some night when Prof. Douglas is sure to be there, and will expect us. It was more than interesting, we thought, merely to have seen the exterior of an observatory where so much noted work has been done.

We both enjoyed our trip to the Cliff-Dwellings so much. I almost had to pinch myself when at last we stood within one, to realize that we were not only dreaming the dream of many years, but were actually there. I am not going to describe them, for my "few lines" have lengthened more than I had intended, besides Minna intends to, if she hasn't already, and I know she can do far better justice to them than I. I wish you could have seen her face when she first saw that cañon, but maybe she will give you a hint of her feeling at least, herself. It was one of Mr. Corser's ideas that we put off our trip to the Grand Cañon until tomorrow, and take this first, for he and others have said that we would hardly have noticed the cañon of the Cliff-Dwellings, grand and inspiring as it is, if we had seen the other first; as it is, we shall never forget now our double impressions of awe and interest received there that afternoon, and are so thankful for the hint. We have both decided, fully, that if we don't succeed in getting every member of our family out to see this "Wonderland" for themselves, within the next few years, it won't be for the want of trying!

This morning we attended service at the Presbyterian Chapel. It was children's day, with the exercises, speaking, singing, recitations, etc., entirely by the children, of which there were about forty-five. The Sunday School evidently is better attended than the church, from all accounts. There are three Chapels here, the Methodists and

Catholics each having one also, but they say the last is the best attended, as there are more Catholics here. Mrs. Knox says there are no poor people here; that is, none in want for they all seem able to earn, at least, the bare necessities, and that is about all the ambition many of them seem to have. They might have borrowed that disposition from their Indian neighbors, if they had any, but I will mention for Juliette's benefit that not a single "brave" have we seen, in the near vicinity, with the exception of one lonely, slouchy looking old Supi [Supai], who wandered into town the other morning, and he didn't deserve the name. . . .[16]

Minna and Jo left Flagstaff for Grand Canyon the day after these letters were written, returning on July 1 in time for the annual Fourth of July festivities. According to the sisters, Flagstaff and the Fourth of July were made for each other. At last, they would see live "rough riding," probably the first they had witnessed outside of an indoor arena in New York City. Jo wrote to her family:

New Bank Hotel
Flagstaff, Arizona
July 2

What a "feast," as we have had reading [your letters], you can imagine, when you remember how we used to look forward to letters from home while we were abroad. As far as distance is considered, we might almost be abroad here, although we do not in the least feel in a "foreign country," for the return here last night from the Cañon seemed almost like a home coming. There were so many familiar faces here to welcome us and to say that they wondered when we would be back again and then to crown all, the splendid letters from home.

Speaking of foreign countries reminds me that among the letters was one from London, for Minna, which Julie may be interested to learn was from F. W., giving some account of the preparations for the Queen's Jubilee, and hoping Minna would write to her, for she "so loves" to receive letters when away from home.

They are evidently having a fine time, but couldn't possibly be any finer than that we are having. Minna thinks she will be surprised to receive an answer to her letter addressed from Arizona.

Sunday, July 4

I was writing in the parlour when Mrs. and Miss Knox and some friends came in just then and the rest of the evening was spent in talking about Grand Cañon days, theirs in the past, and our just over. . . . Just to think, Papa and Mamma, that eleven years ago today, we spent Sunday, then also the "Glorious Fourth," in San Francisco! I think Minna and I would have opened our eyes if we could have foreseen ourselves then, in the Arizona town of Flagstaff today.

Such an appropriate name, too, for a town in which to spend the day, and I can assure you that they "rally round the Flag" right loyally out here. The Fourth, to be celebrated tomorrow, gives promise of being a day long to be remembered. When we arrived from the Cañon, Thursday evening, enterprising citizens had already planted a row of good sized pine trees (brought from forests near here) along the main street on which the hotel faces, on the other side of which runs the railroad. I believe the street goes by the name of "Front Street"—at least Mrs. Sisson, the friend of Mr. Corser who took us to the Cliff Dwellings, said she thought it was, and a few others asked since, are of the same opinion, although one wasn't sure, for the town is so small that the streets are unnamed and consequently neither houses nor stores are numbered. If your friend "Mrs. Smith" has lived here any length of time, it is known exactly where by everyone in town, and Mrs. S. goes to the post office for her mail so no other address is needed.

I had quite a funny time yesterday afternoon hunting up Minna's and my friend, Mrs. Charles Knoop, the laundry lady, for my first informant pointed almost due West, "the second house down that street" she thought, but the "second house" proved to be uninhabited. The householder next door, after pointing northeast, across a vacant lot, finally started me on the right track.

The pine trees put up for tomorrow's celebration, along the one side-walk of Front Street, reminded us in their sudden growth of those which Mr. Lewis had put up in Bear Creek [Pa.], on either side of the walk up to the Mokwa Inn when he gave his house-warming. They certainly here add very much to the dusty little street, which otherwise is utterly devoid of trees of any kind. Opposite, though, across the railroad, are open prairie-like fields, with forests of pine trees beyond, which form a restful scene to the eye. It is in these fields across the track that the rough riding, the races and other amusements are to take place. A grandstand has been erected, where we may find seats with Mrs. and Miss Knox tomorrow morning, for a near and safe view of the sights. As to "safe" I mean that if some of their "broncos" tear about as they have a way of doing up and down Front Street, we would not prefer to be standing anywhere on the field.

There are to be fireworks, also in the evening, but I cannot tell how they will compare with those which we have so often enjoyed at the Summit. Minna and I have wondered several times today, if the usual celebration will take place at the Hotel [in Glen Summit] tomorrow, and whether you, Nan and Julie, have been more than successful in collecting the money. I don't believe that would be much of an undertaking here, for all seem to have been looking forward for weeks to the celebration tomorrow. As Mrs. Knox said today, they have so few holidays and local amusements here, that the Fourth is looked forward to as a time of great jubilee and jollification, and no one will forget what day it is nor have a sleepy time tomorrow.

The stores, the hotels, of which there are two, and many of the little one and two story wooden houses are gaily decorated with flags and bunting. The dining room of the New Bank is certainly gorgeous, especially as to the ceiling, from the center of which hangs a large "liberty bell" made of bunting over a frame. Its clapper hangs almost over Minna's head, but it looks securely put up and not at all heavy anyway, so we don't worry.

I told her that if it was only covered with flowers it would look very like a wedding bell, but that didn't seem to worry her either! When I made the remark, Mrs. Knox said that there had been two weddings in the parlour, last year, when they were here, but don't be scared, Mamma, in spite of Minna's scientific tastes, I promise you that I shall do my best to prevent her and any "withered old professor" from holding the third wedding in this parlour.

I will confess, however, that we are both on the lookout for "one professor," but please don't be startled, we simply mean the one from New York City, in whose party we might have gone perhaps, but we are ungracious enough to feel more than glad that we didn't, seeing that we have managed so far without him. We are curious, however, as to whether the party started at all, for if they kept to their original plan, according to the Raymond Agent, they should be this way either before this, or very soon now, and they would probably come here, as the Grand Cañon Hotel, which is the name of the other, isn't as good, and most tourists come here.

Many are arriving now from out of town for the celebration of the next two days, fifty are expected tomorrow, for the cut rates on the Atlantic and Pacific for the "C. E." [Christian Endeavor] convention, the special trains for which having been passing through here for the last two days, have brought many to Flagstaff, as well as the celebration.

The rooms are more than taken, and six cots have been put up in the hall while others will be placed in the parlour tonight. It was only by writing some days ahead, from the Cañon, that we managed to secure our room, only one, until after the sixth when they can let us have the second, which joins it. This is a nice, light airy room, with good sized double bed, so we are managing very well.

This morning we went with Mrs. Knox to the Presbyterian Chapel which is a few blocks from here, on another street with no name. The little building is sadly in need of a new coat of paint and Minna and I have been wondering if the possibility may arise before we leave of a subscription being started, towards which we might contribute for a "new coat" for the building. We only wish Mr. Corser felt as anxious for it as we, for it might serve as a chance for us to show our appreciation of all he has done for us. . . .

We sent a telegram to Mamma, the morning after our arrival here from the Cañon, which I hope arrived early on Friday, which after we sent it caused Minna and me to smile at the remembrance of how we had informed you that the "drafts and Kodak" were "both very well."[17]

After returning to Flagstaff from Grand Canyon, Minna described the sisters' earlier trip during their first visit there to a cinder mountain known today as Sunset Crater, situated amid the volcanic field east of Flagstaff.

July 10

When I said that we were going to Sunset Mountain I didn't mean to tell an intentional fib; in fact, on that very morning when we started out I would have told you the same thing. The day began with heavy rolling clouds, a most unusual thing for us to see, though it must happen often enough in the rainy season, now barely commenced. Mrs. and Miss Knox couldn't go and Mr. Corser had asked Mrs. Olney to take their place.[18] The horses had tried to make an impression by running away when there was no one in the carriage, so we kept an anxious eye on the lunch boxes and the ice cream freezer, and I think there was not one of us but would have grabbed that freezer if matters had gone far enough to oblige us to jump out. We were going to have such fun with that ice cream, sitting in the shade of stately pines and resting after our heroic exertions; for Sunset Mountain is a black cinder cone, several hundred feet high, where the saying about "three steps forward and two back" is literally true. They say it takes an interminable time to climb up it and only ten minutes to come down.[19]

But alas for our happy dreams! About a mile out of town the clouds decided that they had not been treating us fairly and began to put in some good hard work. Finally it penetrated to our minds that it wouldn't be a bad idea to put the curtains up, so Mrs. Olney jumped out into the pouring water and proceeded to button them on. Jo and I stayed where we were and fastened up our side of the carriage at the cost of nothing more than a soaked sleeve apiece,— but Mrs. Olney! When she was safely inside and we could again turn our attention to the fiery steeds, she suggested building a fire and warming the ice cream, but we kept right on.

It's good that the landscape no longer distracted our attention, for if we hadn't been able to watch the rise and fall of the horses' heels we might have thought we were not moving. Slow! The poor beasts evidently thought that we had started on a week's camping trip and were saving their strength. So on we jogged, patiently watching where the dull red summit of Sunset Mountain showed faintly between the black peak and the gray sky.

Sunset Mountain takes its name from a narrow rim of fiery rock that makes it look as if the last sunlight of evening was always reddening its top. A good landmark to steer by, you will think, but when you know that not one of the party had ever seen the Sunset Mt. road you may pause and reflect, as we did about twelve miles from home. There was the mountain still distant, with a line of lower hills between us and the hills. There also was the road, stretching out invitingly before us and leading us—where? Plainly away from the mountain! After a little deliberation we decided— what has since proved true—that we were on the Grand Cañon road, a branch that is used in spring when the shorter and more hilly road is impassable. And then we meekly turned back and gave up our first plan, for it was getting late and was too rainy for a view, anyway.[20]

But we weren't going home, oh no. We turned off toward the Old Caves, which are on top of a hill. The ambitious Mr. Corser wanted to go to the New Caves, some six miles farther on, but we managed to convince him that we wouldn't be disappointed if we stopped for lunch then and there. (It was after one o'clock.) So we stopped at the foot of the cave hill, and all the while the rain poured cheerfully down. The aforesaid stately pines do very well as ornaments to the landscape but they are not any great success as umbrellas, therefore we stayed in the carriage.[21]

And wasn't that ice cream good! Never mind the dripping outside, never mind a stray shiver or two, the big piles on our plates disappeared about as fast as if we had really tried Mrs. Olney's plan of warming them over a fire. But when Mr. Corser got out to explore the hill and see if it was the one we wanted, we found that that unfortunate man had been sitting all the morning in a puddle of water!

The rain was kinder to us than we had hoped, for it stopped long enough for us to wash the dishes. Then we took courage and started for the caves.

I don't know whether the Old Caves are altogether artificial or whether they had a natural beginning, but as they appear now they seem to be only a series of rounded holes dug in the loose, porous rock of the volcanic hillside. Back of most of the outside caves there are holes, just big enough to crawl through, opening into little round inner rooms some six feet across. One of those little boxes in the rock isn't a bad place to sit and meditate—if the rest of the party happen to be in another cave.[22]

To think that they lived there, those people of the far-off days when a rough, dark wall curving over their heads, a little diluted daylight coming through a hole in the rocks, and a few pots and baskets were enough to make a home. At least they didn't require either architects or builders; their work must have been more like digging in a well-packed ash pile than anything else, for the red cinder-like rock crumbles and falls in pieces beneath one's fingers.

All around the northern side of the San Francisco peaks the level plain is lumped and roughened with these great cinder heaps from the long extinct craters. Covered with a growth of scrubby piñon and sage brush, they are very good to look at, but when it comes to climbing them—! It is slide, scramble, slip and pull, and nearly half the time you are going in the wrong direction. You can see that it must be rather hard to go up when the only way to keep from going down is to keep still. But when you want to come down it is a different matter. You run, you jump, you slide, you do everything but roll, quite sure that the cinders piling under your feet will stop you sometime, and it's more fun than coasting. In fact, it is a case of "you keep your balance, the mountain does the rest."

We started home, still in the rain, and ate the rest of our ice cream with cut up peaches (scooped up, I should say, since we dug out the pieces with a spoon) beside some Indian ruins. How's that for the wild West? They conduct picnics in style here, for they are all so used to the business. A summer outing doesn't mean new dresses and a crowded hotel, in this part of the country, it means a camping trip.

And now you shall have a rest. . . . And assure the anxious members that we will "keep out of the way of the snakes" even if we have to view the scene from the distance of a second story roof.[23]

Though the arrival of the transcontinental railroad forever changed the West, Flagstaffians themselves have remained much the same during the last one hundred years—spirited, unpuritanical, and persistent stargazers. The main street, today called Santa Fe Avenue, could still be called Railroad Avenue or Front Street because it continues to parallel the railroad track that first brought tourists to Arizona's magnificent Grand Canyon.

Notes

1. These descriptions may be found throughout Arizona tourist brochures of the time, as well as in the *Flagstaff Sun-Democrat*.

2. *Flagstaff Sun-Democrat*, Sept. 2, 1897.

3. Webb, *Tree Rings*, 37; *Flagstaff Sun-Democrat*, April 22, 1897.

4. In 1897 the people of northern Arizona also used the spelling *canyon*. The man most responsible for this ambivalence was author Charles F. Lummis, who loudly opposed in his books and articles the use of *cañon*. For Minna and Jo to have spelled it other than *cañon* in their letters would have been a capitulation to the lost souls who had never been exposed to the Lummis enthusiasm.

5. Mary Willcox Sisson was the wife of Frederick W. Sisson; he worked for Arizona Lumber & Timber Co., formerly Ayer Lumber Co., in Coconino County.

6. The Nineteenth Territorial Legislature, which convened Jan. 18, 1897, ignored the people's petitions for an appropriation to preserve Arizona antiquities. The Arizona Antiquarian Association first funded the conservation of Montezuma Castle in 1897; Frank C. Reid of Flagstaff collected the $500 Minna mentions. Lummis noted that amount collected as "about $150." Lummis, "The Rescue of Montezuma's Castle," 44. Reid accompanied the Hollenback sisters to the Walpi Snake Dance in August 1897.

7. Amelia refers to the Natural Bridge near the town of Pine in Verde Valley. With a span of over 500 feet, the breadth of the bridge is greater than that of Virginia's Natural Bridge. Barnes, *Arizona Place Names*, 110. Since no Hollenback photographs of the Natural Bridge are extant, it is uncertain if the sisters indeed visited the bridge.

8. The Summer School of Science was held by the Northern Arizona Normal School (now Northern Arizona University). The school included departments in music, drama, and natural history, directed by prominent scholars. In July 1896 accommodations for 500 students were made. The Lowell Observatory also taught various scientific courses during the summer, supplemented by popular lectures. Lummis, "Flagstaff, Arizona," 250.

9. In 1897 the three tourist trails leading to the bottom of Grand Canyon were the Bass,

Grand View, and New Hance Trails. The Bright Angel (Cameron), originally an old Havasupai Indian trail to Indian Gardens, didn't reach the bottom of the canyon until around 1902. Pattee, "Flagstaff and the Grand Canyon," 131; Hughes, *In the House of Stone and Light*, 54.

10. The sisters noted two of the three Lummis books they purchased, *The Land of Poco Tiempo* and *The Spanish Pioneers*.

11. ABH to mother, June 13, 1897, HC.

12. On September 16, 1897, a Mrs. W. H. Knox and a Miss Knox, from Wisconsin, accompanied by E. B. Knox, Phoenix, A. T., signed the Bright Angel Hotel register at Grand Canyon. Mrs. Martin Buggeln Collection, MNAL. A business card of a later year in the Hollenback Collection identifies a Claire G. Knox as proprietor of the Ideal Hotel, Flagstaff.

13. P. E. Kipp, San Diego, Calif., signed the Bright Angel register on June 11, 1897. Bright Angel Hotel Register, MNAL.

14. The "Raymond's Vacation Excursions of [W.] Raymond & [I. A.] Whitcomb, 31 East 14th St., New York City," traveled the world over, giving birth to modern tourism. *New York Times*, Mar. 16, 1894; *From Train to Plane: Travelers in the American West*.

15. Double stars (first observed in the seventeenth century) constitute a binary system, sometimes of two or more stars in proximity, which to the naked eye appear as one. Astronomer Thomas J. J. See received his Ph.D. from the University of Berlin in 1892. Webb, *Tree Rings*, 38. The career of Andrew Ellicott Douglass in the fields of astronomy and dendrochronology spanned seven decades. The two disciplines were interrelated in his study of sunspots and their cycles to determine the possible correlation of climatic changes evidenced by tree rings. Archaeologists today date timbers in ruins by this technique developed by Douglass. In 1889 Douglass, a graduate of Trinity College in Hartford, Conn., joined William H. Pickering as an assistant in the Harvard College Observatory; in 1894 Douglass helped amateur astronomer Percival Lowell in a search for an observatory site in Arizona, Flagstaff being the final choice. Groundbreaking ceremonies took place on April 23, 1894, on a hill that became known as Mars Hill. The following year the astronomers concentrated on the search for life on Mars. Lowell's theory of Mars and its "canals" (suggesting some sort of engineering) was erroneously based on a translation of the Italian word *canali*—"channels" or "grooves"—used to describe surface lines on Mars that the Italian astronomer Schiaparelli had discovered in 1877. In the late nineteenth century, after Schiaparelli's failing eyesight forced him to abandon his research, Lowell was eager to continue it. Wide recognition of the theories came about through Lowell's 1895 work, *Mars*, and H. G. Wells's science fiction novel, *The War of the Worlds*. Although the research of Douglass, as principal assistant, was to document Lowell's Martian theory, Douglass also studied Jupiter and its four principal satellites. Ultimately, the theory, which was hotly debated by serious astronomers, would cause a break between Douglass and Lowell in 1901. By 1906 Douglass was on the faculty at the University of Arizona in Tucson after teaching at Northern Arizona Normal School in Flagstaff while simultaneously serving as a Coconino County probate judge. He remained in Tucson, pursuing his tree-ring research and establishing Steward Observatory, until his death in 1962 at age ninety-five. Webb, *Tree Rings*, ix–x, 10, 45–53, 61.

16. JH to mother, June 13, 1897, HC.

17. JH to parents, July 2 to 4, 1897, HC.

18. Mrs. Florence Olney taught grade school in Flagstaff. The Hollenback sisters became very attached to her, calling her "Ma" and corresponding with her for several years following their Arizona trip.

19. Sunset Crater, first named by Maj. John Wesley Powell in 1892, was formed around A.D. 1066 by volcanic eruption. Its colors range from yellow to dull red and finally the

black of volcanic ash. Sunset Crater National Monument was created on May 26, 1930, but according to a sign at the monument, Sunset Crater Trail was closed to the public in April 1973, having worn down to 5-6 feet deep. Barnes, *Arizona Place Names*, 87.

20. The branch road (eastern route) Minna described skirted the east side of the San Francisco Peaks, eventually joining the Fern Mountain route (western route) to Grand Canyon near East Cedar Ranch. See Mangum and Mangum, *Stage Coach Line*, 90–91.

21. On the trip to Sunset Crater, Minna and Jo also visited the Sunset Crater ice caves. These lava caves supplied Flagstaff with ice year-round in the 1880s. Formed by the cooling of surface mass while the molten lava underneath flowed away, the caves capture and retain cold air. Barnes, *Arizona Place Names*, 87; Colton, *The Sinagua*, 37–39, 66–67.

22. These caves are near the Old Caves Crater, several miles south of Sunset Mountain. Coble-Power map in *Land of Sunshine*, 125; Colton, *The Sinagua*, 37–39. See also Mangum and Mangum, *Stage Coach Line*, 74, 88.

23. ABH to mother, undated to July 5 and July 10, 1897, HC.

Chapter Three
John Hance's Grand Old Cañon

As I visited the places where Amelia and Josephine Hollenback camped in 1897 and read their letters emoting about the Arizona sunsets, I sensed their presence and youthful enthusiasm. But it is difficult today to evoke the absolute isolation and quiet they described, with hordes of people in automobiles and campers thronging to view the views, tramp the trails, and run the Colorado River.

Fortunately, a few vestiges of the past remain in secluded places. Many of the same pine trees surround guide John Hance's old campground, their girth displaying the growth of more than a century. Crumbling foundations indicate structures built nearby in later decades. Unfortunate for the visitor of today, this obscure campsite has been long forgotten and is not open to the public. The dusty wagon road leading into it has been replaced by new roads farther west. Grand vistas remain the same, though place-names have changed over time for no apparent reason or were simply misnamed by an early historian. Thanks to the letters of the adventuresome Hollenback sisters, one South Rim promontory has at last reclaimed its original name of Hollenback Point. This point, east of Zuni Point and named in 1897 by John Hance in honor of Amelia and Josephine, became known as Papago Point in 1906. Today, however, Hollenback Point is not accessible to tourists.[1]

Women tourists were few and far between in nineteenth-century Arizona and New Mexico and suitable accommodations just as scarce. Hiring a wagon with a driver and providing water, food, and shelter was often unreliable and expensive, with unforeseen difficulties of every description. It was indeed the only mode of transportation in the nineteenth century to visit most historic sites now reached so easily by automobile. But to Amelia and Josephine, traveling by wagon was not really an ordeal but an unparalleled adventure of the American spirit.

A trip in 1897 to Grand Canyon, Arizona Territory, was memorable enough for two young women from the East, but an all-day ride to and from the bottom of the canyon for ladies tightly laced in corsets made a "breath-taking" trip even more so. Camping outdoors or sitting astride a mule was not every woman's ideal vacation. However, to the wealthy and very proper Misses Hollenback, who chose to straddle their mounts in ankle-length, divided skirts rather than bloomers, northern Arizona during the summer of 1897 became a campground of pure joy.[2]

Grand Canyon tourists arrived at the Atlantic & Pacific Railroad station in downtown Flagstaff. The station stood across the main street from the red-sandstone New Bank Hotel, where Minna and Jo stayed between treks. The Bank Hotel, which occupied the second floor over a bank, had added "New" to its name after a recent refurbishing. Proprietor Lyman H. Tolfree saw to it personally that the Hollenback ladies lacked nothing that might be only a few steps away, particularly money.[3]

J. Wilbur Thurber called himself the "gentlemanly" driver of the early morning stage that ran between Flagstaff and the South Rim of Grand Canyon. Amelia and Josephine failed to mention the name of their particular driver. The stage route wound northward up through mammoth pine trees and across Hart Prairie to the area of lush Fern Mountain. The first relay station, by 1897 an alternate at Little Spring, meant fresh horses and cold buttermilk or other refreshment among white-barked aspen trees, wild flowers, and green ferns watered by melting snows of the towering San Francisco Peaks nearby.[4]

From the 8,000-foot rest stop, people and horses began the downhill dash to East Cedar Ranch, thirty-five miles from Flagstaff, beyond the cinder-coned Missouri Bill Hill.[5] After arriving at East Cedar Ranch in midday, dusty passengers ate a 50-cent meal in the middle of nowhere dotted with cedar trees. The stage route headed again northward via Rabbit Canyon to Lockwood Tank, then on to Moqui Station, a final stop and horse change before reaching Grand Canyon. Then just at sunset, the swaying stage lurched over the brow of one last incline and down into a secluded rim-site of tent houses and camp smoke.

Minna wrote to her childhood friend Mabel Haddock in Glen Summit, where the Hollenbacks summered in the house they called "The Cottage":

June 21, 1897

Oh if you could see us now! We are sitting in a most palatial canvas residence with a wooden floor and a Navajo blanket for a rug, two beds, three chairs, a Sibley stove in one corner, a washstand and what passes for a dressing table.[6] Also three nails in the tent poles, at present decorated with the new cowboy hats which are the joy of our hearts. If that isn't a picture of luxury, I don't know where you will find one. Only the ignorant would call this camping out. Why, we have course dinners served in a large log-house, and there is a parlor next to the dining room. We expect to try real camping in about two weeks, the kind where you travel by wagon or horseback and take your own outfit. A lady whom we met in Flagstaff wants to go to the Natural Bridge [in Verde Valley] or Cataract Cañon [in Grand Canyon] and will probably ask us to join her party.

Please don't think that I am using this pencil just to show you what a variety of writing materials a person can have, seventy miles from a railroad. The ink in my fountain pen has given out and I left the rest in Flagstaff. My pen was filled only a short while ago, but the air in this thirsty country is so dry that it drinks up anything, even ink.

When we left you standing on the platform at Glen Summit and had said good-bye to our people at Wilkes-Barre, I looked out at the dear green hills and felt as homesick as if my eyes were already straining over the hot wavering sands of an Arizona desert. But now that we are here, I have only one wish in the world, and that is somehow, anyhow, to bring the rest of you here too. Oh Mabel, they miss the greatest amount of grandeur and beauty that could gladden the sight of anyone's whole lifetime, who have not seen this place. We think we know the meaning of those two words, but a person has no idea of their greatness until he stands by the brink of the Cañon. There is no use in calling it a wonder, or anything of that kind. Those words do not seem to mean much here, and yet we have to use them or else keep still. That is why I am not going to describe any part of the Cañon. No one could.

If we could drive around Glen Summit in the imposing style in which we came out here, people would think we were grand duchesses or some other royal personages. The stages are big lumbering affairs with canvas tops and room for seven people beside the driver. (Not on the same seat, though that sounds like it.) Generally, they use four horses, sometimes six, but when we came through they had to do something a little out of the ordinary. So they fastened a big horse on one side of the wheelers and a little colt trotted along on the other side, and there we were with four horses abreast and two more in front of them. Add to this a clumsy, swinging stage, a few ruts in the road and remember that we were on a seat with springs of its own, and you will have some idea of our feelings as part of that cavalcade. It was good practice for horseback riding.

The system of road making in this country is beautifully simple. One man drives over the hills, another drives in the first man's tracks and that is a road. The Grand Cañon road is something more pretentious than that and is often used by wheelmen [bicyclists], but there is a grain or two of dust on it. Part of the time we could not see the wheelers, and by the time we reached the dinner station we might have passed for Indians in war paint by just using a handkerchief to make a few white streaks on our faces.[7]

If there were no Cañon and no stage line, it would be worth anyone's while to come here and talk to John Hance. He is the greatest man in all this part of the country, owns the whole Cañon and everyone in it—though I doubt if he has a deed to any large piece of it and is a sort of grandfather or uncle to everyone around him. Years ago he was a scout and went through all the Indian wars, but took to lumbering only a few months before he might have been killed with Custer on the Little Big Horn. Then a cowboy told him of the Grand Cañon, in days when people hardly knew of its existence, and he came out here in the middle of winter and was, I think, the first white man to climb down its awful walls and stand beside the Colorado River.[8] Now he lives here, as he has for thirteen years, and spends his summer taking people over his trails; and I never saw a person whom I would rather trust with any number of children on a trail or my whole fortune if I had one to be left somewhere. He is as patient, kind-hearted, thoughtful and unselfish a man as you can imagine, if he does have a peculiar and original way of pronouncing his English; but, oh my, what fish stories he can tell! You can depend on his word to the end when he is serious, but it would take a mind-reader to tell whether he is serious or not. That is why it is worth a long journey to hear him talk. To hear him tell his big yarns is more fun than any number of boxes of monkeys. Everyone within a radius of a few hundred miles knows John Hance, and I couldn't resist saying a few words about a genuine old-fashioned pioneer and frontiersman, such as we read about but don't often come across.[9]

Last Wednesday we went down the new Hance trail to the river, and no one could forget five minutes of the day when he first did that. "A mile and a quarter you go into the solid earth, and if you put your ear to the ground by the river you can hear the Chinamen eating rice with their chopsticks." (Quotation from Captain Hance.) The trail is very good, and there is only one place where people nearly always walk and lead their mules because, as Mr. Hance says, it "looks a leetle frightful." But it is an experience to make an innocent Easterner think that she has accomplished something quite wonderful, till she finds that John Hance and his men think nothing of going to the river and back twice a day.[10]

Do you know how wide a mule is? I don't believe you ever will until you try riding one all day on a man's saddle, up and down at about the same angles as if you were jumping a row of five foot fences. Most of the time the trail is like the longer zigzag path by the glen falls; sometimes it is like the short path that we use, and then you stand up and brace yourself back in your saddle, but the next minute you are leaning forward, frantically clutching the pommel and wondering if the mule thinks you are nailed to the saddle. And all the time your sister is laughing at you and telling you what you look like, and the worst of it is that you know it is all true.

After a while you find that there was no need of holding on and you begin to think of going down the trail next day on a bicycle, and one lasting result of the day's trip is sure to be a great respect for anyone who could make so secure a way of descent down places where it would seem as if only lizards could find a pathway. There has only been one accident in the Cañon, and that was when a man was killed by lightning [in 1895].

When we went down I rode a mule by the dear familiar name of Fatty, which was very easy to remember, but every time someone said "Get along, Fatty," it gave me an unpleasant start. She deserved her name, too, but the way that plump animal could climb was a wonder. Give her a place big enough to set her feet and she didn't care particularly whether it was level or sideways or upside down.

Jo, who was just behind me, had a slow and thoughtful mule with a fondness for admiring the view, and every time we came to a narrow ledge barely wide enough for the trail, Mr. Hance would call back, "The trail forks here and you'll be lost if you don't hurry up." It is wonderful what an appreciation these mules have of scenery. At the top of every steep place they stop and gaze around as if they wanted to stay all night.

We left the hotel about half past seven and went down, down till I thought we must have reached the middle of the earth, and Mr. Hance remarked that we were "half way down and it was gettin' a little freezin'." In winter when there is five feet of snow at the rim of the Cañon, Mr. Hance moves down to the bottom and spends a few months in what he says is "the finest winter climate in the world," but in summer it is a place to get a new brick complexion, warranted to last a week.

When I come home you need never give me any more Huyler's candy. Only show me a glass of Glen Summit water and that will be enough. I thought I learned something about water in the three days' water famine we once had in Brooklyn, but I never knew half its value till I came to this country where water makes men's fortunes and lack of water keeps settlers away. There is good drinking water, but very little for anything else. They have a habit of carrying some around with them whenever they go anywhere, and a sip out of an old canteen is more of a luxury than all the ice cream in the world, even in that stone oven of a Cañon.

Remember, you must not call the Cañon an oven, though the bottom would make a first class one on some days. When we were there it was positively cool, sitting in the shade, listening to Mr. Hance's stories and drinking lemonade, and the sun was only warm enough to make one sure it was there.

We have been here just a week today, and I wouldn't give that week for an ordinary year. We may stay till next Saturday (this is Monday) and sometimes I do pity the people who only stay two days as most of them do, but again I want to congratulate them for being so supremely fortunate as to have that much.

This is stage day and a very important occasion. The stage comes at about sunset, so that people first see the Cañon at the most beautiful hour of the day. If you were on the stage, you would be rocking along a bumpy road through a beautiful pine forest when the driver would tell you to "keep a sharp lookout through the trees to the right and you'll see the glen." (Glen! They have large ideas in the West!) You look, and catch a few glimpses of the sunshine on some pink cliffs, and wonder where in the forest around you they could have managed to hide a cañon sixteen miles wide and 6,600 feet deep.

Then the stage goes plunging down a hill and there in front of you is a little piney hollow and a settlement of about fourteen tents, a log house and a cabin with apparently a small crowd of people standing around watching for the stage. The sight of those people makes you suddenly remember the thick layer of dust with which you are decorated, and you wish you could get out on the other side; then you wonder if that "benevolent old Yankee" leaning over the fence is John Hance.

In a few minutes you start to walk up the sandy slope back of the house. There are many-colored rock fragments strewed around, and wild flowers and cacti, sage brush and queer twisted cedars and piñons grow all about. Perhaps if you stood on those rocks just ahead you might see better which way to go. You try it, and then you see IT! As if half the world had fallen away before your feet, and after that you are no longer on the same old earth.[11]

If you were one of the watchers at stage time instead of an arrival, you would almost think that the only person here was Mr. Clayton, the manager! He is a hard-worked youth with a smile or rather a perpetual grin who stands by while you are at the table and moves the dishes so that you can easily reach them. A manager passing the bread? Yes, for the manager is also the waiter, hotel clerk, porter, photographic assistant and I don't know what else. Quite a list of occupations for one person, isn't it? On stage nights he rushes around in a way that would give an acrobat points. Couldn't you borrow someone's flying machine and come out here for a few hours? Please excuse these smutty sheets and I will try to do better next time.[12]

Like her Grand Canyon mule, Minna Hollenback was also affectionately known as "Fatty" at home. Her playful sisters continually teased her about weight, and though her figure demanded an extra tug with corset laces, her intellect had already begun to yearn for freedom from such social constraints, as she hints in this letter to an older sister:

> *Grand Cañon Camp*
> *Arizona*
> *June 21*

There is going to be a chance for us to use our pistols [the bon voyage gifts]. On the fourth of July they are going to have a grand celebration in Flagstaff, with prize bronco riding, steer catching and all the rest of it.

Since our large and varied experience on cañon trails, Jo and I have decided that that is just the opening we want, and as no professional cowgirl travels without fire arms, you have saved us that expense.

A rival of Buffalo Bill's wanted to bring his Wild West show to Flagstaff and give an exhibition on the Fourth, but as one Flagstaffian remarked, this is the wild West and the showmen could give them no novelty unless it was an Effete East show; so the inhabitants declined and are going to keep to home talent. Lest you treat our pretensions to fame as mere ambitious bubbles, let me inform you that I, your sister, was the first woman to go over John Hance's new trail to Moran Point, and Jo was the second.

Take that in, imagine us climbing awful steeps and leaping terrific chasms; and then I will relieve your feelings by telling you that it is a very good trail along the rim and our being first was only a case of "first come, first served." Heretofore, people have been obliged to reach Moran Point by an inside trail with no view, and it is true that we were the foremost members of the first party who ever saw the trail along the edge. Only the builder was before us, and we will point it out with pride when you come and find all the trails old and well-travelled, though come to think of it, that is not likely to happen in John Hance's day. He is always planning new ones, so you may be a pioneer yet.

- - - -That means the arrival of the stage, containing Papa's letter of the 15th to Jo and yours of the 16th. Also five or six other people, who don't count. We took the letters up on the rocks and read them with the sun watching us over a far point of rock, and the whole wonder of sunset in the Cañon going on at our very feet. And now I wish you to understand that the next time you send your love to "Fatty," I shall think you mean my friend the mule and shall feel left out in the cold.

If anyone is surprised to see the enclosed bill coming home when it might have stayed at the Cañon, tell them that it is the bill for my broad shoes that I use for climbing, though Burt wouldn't recognize them now, and say that it came to Mama because at Burt's [in Brooklyn] I always have things charged to Mrs. J. W. Hollenback.

Those same broad shoes, and my short [ankle length] skirt, are the greatest comforts in life. Our everyday attire consists of shirt waists, short skirts, old shoes and flapping felt hats, regular cowboy style. For evening dress we put on long skirts, but we don't assume such style every night. Dear me no, only on stage days to impress the new arrivals with the civilized ways of camp life. It is such fun to put on benevolent airs as the "oldest inhabitants" and dispense second-hand information as if we were the original discoverers of the place.

There was another Lummis enthusiast here the other day, and to hear him talk was absolutely refreshing; and oh, you should come to this place where people speak as if the Natural Bridge and Montezuma's Well were in their back yards.

I am disgusted!! You may have wanted to chop the butcher into little bits, but tomorrow they will have to put me into the corral for safety. Other people's safety, I mean, if this goes on much longer. The people who came tonight don't half appreciate their privileges. They haven't done anything dreadful, but they are as cold as the ice cave in Flagstaff and it is enough to make one glower continually to think that such obtuseness could exist in America. Oh for a sight of the Lummis enthusiast! Some people ought to have a Waldorf on wheels trundled around after them when they go travelling.

Some day I am going to write you a letter if you think you can survive it, but this was only intended to send a few lines of business by tomorrow's stage.[13]

Twenty-nine-year-old Jo teased her half-sister, Juliette, at sixteen the youngest of the Hollenbacks, who stayed behind on the 1897 adventure. Of the six sisters, creative and beautiful Juliette should have been the one to travel with Amelia. Together, they lovingly and vicariously pretended a world of feminine impossibilities to be mastered by women of another century, a world where women were equal to men in politics and other endeavors.

In Camp
Grand Cañon of the
Colorado, Arizona
June 20, 1897

My dear "little Julie"!

Just think, I am too far away from you to chase me upstairs now for calling you that, besides there are no stairs here, unless I should try some of the rocky steps on the trail in the Cañon. I am quite sure you could catch me there, unless I was mounted on the nimble footed "Kitty," the latter I will tell about a little later, for I want you to make her acquaintance, in case you were inclined to believe that your big sister lacked a reasonable amount of courage when she climbed those same "steps" in the Cañon last Wednesday.

Well! "little Julie," if you will forgive me this time I'll "promise not to do it again"; it was only "to pay" you for not having plunged into the wilderness with us. You should have come, you really should, for not a tarantula have we met, neither has a single "sidewinder" dared to cross our path! Minna says to tell you that she has almost forgotten what a "pidie" [centipede] looks like, and she is thinking of coming to Glen Summit to find out. The only excitement in the line of zoology, which we might be able to offer you, would be little lizards and big lizards of several brilliant hues, and an occasional glimpse perhaps of a fat horned-toad.[14]

There were three of the latter around the door of the log house the other morning, the two smaller ones were the loveliest shade of salmon pink, while the great-grandfather toad rejoiced in a skin of the loveliest shade of pale grey, spotted with blue.

But the most interesting zoological specimen here perhaps is "Kitty," at least you may think so, when you hear what was the first thing I learned about her last Wednesday morning. It was 7:30 a.m. and we were ready to start on our all-day trip down John Hance's new trail to the river. As we were apportioned our studs, "Kitty" fell to my lot. Now "Kitty," I would have you understand, is a very innocent-looking brown mule, so I might have been surprised as old "Capt." Hance helped me into the saddle to hear him say that "Kitty had killed thirteen people, and had landed nine more in the County Hospital. Besides she was noted for having tossed eleven young ladies into the trees." "Now come, Kitty," he added, when I was fairly in the saddle, "and make an even dozen of this one!" How is that for an acrobatic Western mule?

Some of the courage I would have you think I possessed I might lay claim to, if old John Hance wasn't noted for being the greatest Western romancer, in a book or out of it. He is so good natured and so full of fun, he would do anything for anyone, and his very yarns make him very amusing. He has lived here at the Grand Cañon for thirteen years, the eleventh of this month, he says. He calls that his "birthday" for he loves the Grand old Cañon so, that he evidently considers that his life before he came here doesn't count. He built the first trail to be used to the river, zigzag down 6,600 feet, "one mile and a quarter," he says, "into the solid earth . . . ."[15]

The morning after we arrived here we sent for him to make arrangements for his taking us to the river the following day. He has one guide in his employ, who sometimes conducts the parties, and a very good guide, too, we were told, but everyone tries to get "old John" himself if possible, so we were not going to go with anyone less noted than himself, if it could be arranged. When we asked him if he could take us down, he replied, "Sure thing!" (a favorite expression of his), "but I can't promise to bring you back!" and then in a very solemn and serious tone— "there's many a poor sole has never come back from that river!" After our first gasp, we assured him that our shoe leather was of the strongest, and as it happened we used very little of it anyway on that trip, though no doubt "Kitty" and Minna's mule lost many a layer from their shoe soles.

There! I mustn't forget to tell you that Minna was barely mounted on her mule, when she was somewhat startled to hear the other guide (who went part ways down the Cañon with us) calling out behind her—"Get up, Fatty! Get up, Fatty!!"—for that was the name of her mule! How we laughed over it, and it struck us as funny every once in a while on the trip. Such a nice old brown "Fatty" as she was anyway. As for the other dear, old (?) "Fatty," she wasn't brown when we got back that night, but the loveliest shade of deep, rich crimson! Even your pale, old sister boasted of red cheeks for once. We are very proud of our good Western color, and do hope it won't, any of it, wear off before we get home. Of course we would be willing to have it a shade or two browner, as it has already grown.

We think you all would have laughed if you could have seen us Wednesday morning as we started off wearing our short golfing and bicycle skirts and broad, Western felt hats (the only kind for the Cañon) mounted astride on our mules![16] We only needed a heavy "six-shooter" stuck into either side of our belts to have made us look like a pair of regular cowboys! Anyway Minna's erect carriage, as she rode in front of me, reminded me of "Buffalo Bill!"

By the way, during his first pow-wow with us the day after we arrived, John Hance told us several tales of his Western life before he came to the Cañon. He knew "Buffalo Bill" very well and at one time he worked with General Custer, and left his employ only about a year before the latter was killed; in fact in "old John's" own words he, John Hance, "punched the breeze just in time to save his own topknot." To "punch the breeze," I would inform you, is dignified Western vernacular for "to escape."[17]

By the time we get home we will have a choice collection of Western phrases, no doubt, for although the "Captain," as he is called, doesn't indulge in them constantly by any means, still I think, being of a kindly nature himself and remembering that we are from the East, he wants us to get the worth of our money and not miss any of the attractions and accomplishments which the West may have to offer. Well! Although he is a "feature" here, and a very funny, kind-hearted and interesting one as well, I mustn't quite fill my letter with him!

Such a glorious ride as we had, down those 6,600 feet on Wednesday; the view ahead, to right and to the left, changed with nearly every step, and each seemingly grander than the last. The trail is John Hance's second one, for the first (where one had to climb down rope ladders, over high precipices part of the way) has been abandoned on account of a bad wash-out in a heavy storm. This new trail is much better. We walked a little (leading our mules) going down, but coming back, there was only one place where it was so steep that we had to dismount.

We reached the river, a rushing muddy torrent, confined by high cliffs, except where the camp is, about one o'clock. The "camp" on its bank consists of one tent and a corral for the horses, but farther down the river John Hance has a little cabin, where he goes with his mules and horses when winter comes on, and it grows too cold to stay up here on the rim of the Cañon.

That may serve to give you some idea of the depth of this "Grand old Glen," as our driver on the stage, coming here, called it. Minna said if this was a "glen," she was going to call ours at the Summit a "cañon," hereafter.

How I wish you could have been with us as we sat on the ground under the trees in front of the tent, down there, in the very "mouth of the cannon!" If Cousin Em could have seen how very comfortable we were, eating our lunch, drinking out of big water canteens, and listening to the roar of the Colorado River, she wouldn't have worried about the "mouth of the cannon" any longer.[18]

We had our cameras and took several views while we were down there. In fact, we have about lived with our cameras either in our hands or strapped to our saddles, for there is some grand view we want to take where ever we turn. Although my little one, the "Pocket Kodak," "punched the breeze" at Fort Leavenworth, I haven't missed it here, for the distances are too great to make that of any use, though I was sorry enough to [have] lost it.

Though by no means an expert yet, I find that I understand my big one much better now than I ever hoped to be able to, and really think I have a few results already which may merit the name of photos. Minna, I know will have some splendid ones. She changes her plates in the dining room of the log house when it is dark enough in the evening. She has been able to use her tripod several times, though when we have been off on trails she has gone without it usually.[19]

Speaking of "trails," we have been somewhat amused to find that nearly every path is a "trail" out here, no matter how short it may be. Hereafter, on our return to Glen Summit, if we have occasion to go to the stable, we will go up the "trail" to reach it.

Our second trail ride was last Friday, when a party of six of us, including old John Hance for guide, took our lunch and water canteens and rode to Moran Point, about four miles away, and after spending some time there, on to Bissell [Zuni] Point, where we had our lunch and returned in the afternoon. From both of these points are to be had some of the grandest views of the Cañon. It was from

Point Moran that Thomas Moran painted his noted picture of the Grand Cañon, now in the Capitol at Washington.[20] Right in front of the Point, is a good sized flat pillar of rock, connected to the main point by only a narrow saddle of rocks, and on this flat, isolated fortress are the remains of some cliff-dwellings, nearly destroyed, however, by wicked vandals who have thought it "fun" to pull down the stones of those priceless relics and roll them over the cliff, just to hear them as they bounce from rock to rock on their way down into the Cañon. Isn't it a shame? Probably no other human family on this earth ever had a finer, grander view from their "front door" than those same prehistoric cliff-dwellers saw whenever they stepped to theirs.

John Hance has a little cabin up here on the rim, about half a mile away, where he goes after the log house here is closed in the fall and it is yet too warm to go down into the Cañon, and from the yard of his log cabin may be had a view of the Cañon nearly as grand as that from Moran Point. His way, however, of telling us that he enjoyed it was to say, that whenever he was hungry for breakfast he went to his cabin door and looked at the Cañon, and that when he wanted some dinner, he went and looked at the Cañon and so on. However, Minna and I have noticed that he has been able to dispose of quite an amount of "chuck" on our trail tours in spite of his remarks. "Chuck," my dear child, is Western for "grub"; more politely termed food or eatables. . . .

We had a fine ride on horseback this morning four miles and a half up the Cañon to the head of Cameron's Trail [Grand View] and coming back we actually cantered several times, about half a mile at a stretch, at least Minna did, and I managed to "stick on" my horse and follow her, head down and elbows out, no doubt, and a pretty and very graceful picture I must have made, as I and the earth didn't come in contact. I feel consequently somewhat elated. Minna's horse was graced by the name of "Sabine," while mine gloried in that of "Alexander," and although Minna's could "sing" such a lovely song that we nicknamed her "Trilby," mine had true general-like instincts and never wanted "Sabine" to get ahead of him.

Minna and I saw the sunset of all we have ever seen the very grandest, from our favorite rocks last night. Please tell Nan it was equal to the "August sunset" she will remember at Glen Summit, some years ago, and to imagine if she can, that overhead, and the Grand Cañon beneath us, a sight we have pictured in our minds forever. . . .[21]

In 1897 the Hollenback sisters ranged in age from thirty-eight to sixteen years, the difference in age often causing an older sister or half-sister to seem more like a mother. These bright, loving women possessed an emotional dependency on one another typical of the time. Their letters to one another poured out intimate thoughts and emotions veiled from those not part of the family network. Inveterate travelers, they wrote hundreds of letters from around the world. During their journeys, they wore the clothing of the era, attire not designed for traveling comfort. Long skirts with blouses buttoned to the neck required enormous physical stamina, particularly for a desert camping endeavor. Despite any discomfort caused by unsuitable dress, Minna and Jo always managed to view their Southwest experiences with humor. The girls' enthusiasm for the magnificent vistas of the Southwest never waned during the summer of 1897, and they became part of its early feminine history.

Notes

1. See Chapter 4, n. 11, for additional information on the renaming of the point.

2. "Many women make the trip [into Grand Canyon]. Very often they discard their skirts and attire themselves in a bloomer style of trousers, the better to clamber about on the rocks and abrupt trails." Clipping from *Arizona Enterprise*, June 9, 1892, John Hance File, AHS. See also McCroskey, ed., *Summer Sojourn to the Grand Canyon*. Some of the same Arizona experiences and people appear in Stella Dysart's diary as in the Hollenback letters.

3. The Bank Hotel Building (McMillan Bldg.) stands today at the corner of Santa Fe Avenue and Leroux Street (Gold and Railroad Avenues in 1897). Originally built in the late 1880s by Thomas Forsythe McMillan, a nephew of President James K. Polk, the first floor housed a Wells Fargo office and the Flagstaff Opera House. Stages to Grand Canyon regularly stopped there. The building is listed both as a national and state historic building. National Register of Historic Places Inventory-Nomination Form, May 2, 1977, NPS; Arizona State Inventory of Historic Places, Coconino Co., ASP.

4. According to the Hollenback sisters, who made references to specific "stage days," it appears that the stagecoach was not yet running daily to Thurber's Camp. The original log-cabin stage relay stop presently stands at Fern Mountain Ranch and is privately owned today; the ranch is 18 miles from Flagstaff. Wahmann, "Grand Canyon Stage Line," 33; National Register of Historic Places Inventory-Nomination Form, Fern Mountain, Oct. 27, 1977, NPS. The alternate relay station in 1897 was Little Spring, a short distance north of Fern Mountain Ranch. Mangum and Mangum, *Stage Coach Line*, 38–39, 90.

5. Missouri Bill Williams (William Sherley Williams, 1787–1849) was a noted mountain-man and fur trapper. A gaunt, red-haired North Carolinian, Williams first visited Arizona in 1837. Barnes, *Arizona Place Names*, 63; McGehee, "Rough Times in Rough Places," 771. Cedar Ranch is owned today by the Babbitts, one of the early northern Arizona families and organizers of the Babbitt Brothers Trading Company, with headquarters in Flagstaff. Cline, *They Came to the Mountain*, 238.

6. Henry Hopkins Sibley, a confederate general who led the invasion of New Mexico Territory in 1862, invented the Sibley conical army tent and stove. Lowe, *Five Years a Dragoon*, 3 n. 1.

7. After a stage trip to Grand Canyon in 1898, world traveler and lecturer Burton Holmes wrote that when a coach was too crowded, a trailer was added, and "Unhappy are the mortals who become inmates of that trailer; they assiduously collect all the dust, their view is cut off by the forward coach, and they see little else." Holmes, *Travelogues*, 12:129.

8. Without question, the most colorful and beloved figure ever to live at Grand Canyon was John Hance. Whether he was the "first white man" to descend into Grand Canyon, as Minna wrote, is questionable.

9. According to the decennial Federal Census, Arizona Territory, Hance was born in 1841 in Tennessee, where the Hance family resided at Cowan's Ferry. As early as 1886, John Hance advertised his ability to accommodate and accompany tourists at Grand Canyon. *Arizona Champion*, Sept. 18, 1886. At one time, John Hance did in fact own 160 acres along the east rim of Grand Canyon, which he homesteaded in 1884; the Hance acreage, however, is not listed in the index of the Coconino Co. Homestead Records. On Nov. 1, 1895, Hance sold his Hance Trail, "commencing at a point of the rim of the Grand Canyon of the Colorado River about one half mile east of the Grand Canyon Hotel and at the Hance Cabin . . . together with that certain spring of water and rock cabin known as the Hance Spring and Rock Cabin situated beside said trail about three miles from the starting point thereof" for $1,500 to J. W. Thurber, owner of the Grand Canyon Stage Line, J. H. [L.] Tolfree, owner of the New Bank Hotel in Flagstaff, and I. F. Wheeler, all of Coconino County. In the contract Hance stipulates that he "will not at any time hereafter, engage in the business of guide at any point within thirty miles of the said Grand Canyon Hotel . . . and that I will not use or permit to be used my name as guide or in connection with the business of guiding tourists, nor in connection with any trail," agreeing to forfeit his quarter interest in the Red Canyon Trail (which became the New Hance Trail) if he did so. By 1897 Hance was again leading tourists into and around Grand Canyon by virtue of a Release signed in 1895 canceling the covenant to compete. Hance retained his possessory rights, receiving a Patent on Feb. 25, 1907. Mangum and Mangum, *Stage Coach Line*, 33, 37. On Mar. 11, 1907, Martin Buggeln, who earlier had sold his Bright Angel Lodge to the Santa Fe Railway, purchased the 160-acre Hance homestead and "the 'Hance' or Red Canyon Trail leading from said premises to the Colorado River" for $5,000 from John Hance. CCR, Deed Book 32:595. In 1908 Buggeln built a 17-room frame hotel adjacent to the old Hance cabin, intending to operate it as a stage station. The arrival of the railroad put a stop to the stages and shifted the tourist area to the west, where it remains today. The National Park Service on Dec. 15, 1947, exercised an option assigned in 1942 by Mrs. Eva Buggeln Moss, paying her $50,000 for the Hance acreage. *Arizona Republic*, Aug. 3, 1948, John Hance File, AHS; CCR, Deed Book 2:567–69; Mrs. Martin Buggeln Coll., MNAL. Ownership of the property by the Park Service ensured the right-of-way for a rim road from Grand Canyon Village to Desert View, the eastern park boundary. The historic Hance log cabin (built by 1889, according to George Wharton James) as well as the two-story Buggeln Hotel were still standing when the Park Service purchased the property in 1947 and in use as part of a cattle-ranching operation. The Service announced it would preserve these structures as historic sites. They were torn down, however, allegedly for safety reasons, around 1960, before the National Historic Preservation Act was passed in 1966. A notation in John Hance's Visitor's Book indicates the "Log Hotel" was dedicated Aug. 6, 1896. Hance died Jan. 16, 1919, and is buried in Pioneer Cemetery near El Tovar Hotel. James, *Grand Canyon of Arizona*, 258; Frances Hance Rose to Lon Garrison, July 31, 1948, GCRL; John Hance, Clipbook, AHS; Euler to author, Dec. 27, 1987; Barnes, *Arizona Place Names*, 145; Woods, ed., *Personal Impressions of the Grand Cañon*, 101.

10. John Hance walked over 70 miles in 1897 from Grand Canyon to Flagstaff in one day. He offered a standing wager, without any apparent takers, of the "sun to sun" hike from the Canyon rim to the Bank Hotel. *Flagstaff Sun-Democrat*, Aug. 5, 1897; Rose to Garrison, GCRL. In seven hours John Hance once made a round-trip to the Colorado River just to rescue a purse left in the bottom of Grand Canyon by one of his lady tourists. Rose to Garrison, GCRL.

11. The first view of the Canyon produced a similar effect on others, as well. In 1902 Charles Lummis wrote, "And from the hotel you climbed a little slope for a hundred yards or so and on a sudden, unforeseen as death tomorrow, the earth fell away before your feet and you were upon the very brink of the noblest scene in the world." Lummis, "A Week of Wonders," 24.

12. ABH to Mabel Haddock, undated [June 21, 1897], HC.

13. ABH to Anna, undated [June 21, 1897], HC.

14. At least 44 species of amphibians and reptiles may be found at Grand Canyon. Whitney, *Field Guide to the Grand Canyon*, 304.

15. John Hance's "birthday" of his arrival at Grand Canyon, according to Jo's letter, would have been June 11, 1884. In a notice placed in the *Arizona Champion*, Jan. 22, 1887, Hance certified that "on or about the 15th day of June, 1884, I took possession of and located as a home that certain unsurveyed Public Land . . . near the place where a trail known as 'Hance Trail' leads down into the Grand Canyon."

16. In 1898 Burton Holmes wrote: "The only lady in our little band of bold adventurers must bow to the strict rules of Captain Hance and don divided skirts, for the old guide will have no ladies in his train who will not ride astride." Hance kept an extra skirt on hand for anyone who came unprepared. Holmes, *Travelogues*, 156. By 1906 divided skirts and straw hats could be rented at El Tovar and Grand View Hotels. Higgins, *Titan of Chasms*, 32.

17. Buffalo Bill Cody led a group of Englishmen to Grand Canyon in 1892. *Flagstaff Coconino Sun*, Nov. 10, 1892; Wetmore, *Last of the Great Scouts*, 270. General George Armstrong Custer was killed in Montana at the battle of Little Bighorn in 1876. It is unlikely that Hance was in Custer's employ as late as 1875, as Jo wrote, because he had already arrived in Arizona by 1869, appearing on the 1870 decennial Federal Census for Arizona.

18. Regarding the phrase "the mouth of the cannon," Josephine was making fun of Cousin Em. The word *cañon* (Spanish variant of canyon) is pronounced "cannon" without the tilde over the "n."

19. Glass plates were the established format used for photographic negatives rather than film, which in 1897 was still in its infancy.

20. In 1874 Congress purchased Thomas Moran's painting of Grand Canyon entitled, *Chasm of the Colorado*, for $10,000. It was hung in the Senate lobby with *The Grand Canyon of the Yellowstone*, also painted by Moran. *Appletons' Cyclopaedia of American Biography*, 4:387; Wilkins, *Thomas Moran*, 93.

21. ABH to Juliette, June 20, 1897.

Chapter Four
Punching the Breeze on the Rim

In the words of Grand Canyon's first guide and storyteller, John Hance, ladies were "punching the breeze" (Western vernacular for "escaping") on the South Rim for a number of years before Minna and Jo Hollenback arrived in 1897. However, these early women did not leave historians the quantity of letters and photographs that the Hollenbacks did. Thus their trip is particularly significant regarding women at Grand Canyon in the nineteenth century.

There were other women who left their mark in Canyon history. Emma Augusta Burbank Ayer, wife of Edward E. Ayer of Chicago, in 1885 became the first woman tourist to descend the Old Hance Trail into Grand Canyon with the aid of ropes. She survived the trip in far better physical condition than her male companions, according to a Flagstaff newspaper. One of her companions was John Hance, who first descended Grand Canyon in 1874. "On Sunday, the 10th inst., Mr. Ed E. Ayer, wife and daughter, Henry Ayer, Miss Sturgis, Mr. and Mrs. A. A. Dutton, Major Miner and Dr. Lightfoot started from Flagstaff for the Grand Canon . . . Mr. and Mrs. Ed Ayer and Henry Ayer went down to the bottom of the canon, and were three days making the trip. Mrs. Ayer is the first lady who ever attempted the trip."[1]

Arizona pioneer Bert Cameron recounted that the second white woman to go to the Colorado River was Mrs. Annie M. Cameron (his mother) in 1889. Another woman in early Canyon history was Sarah Allen Doyle. According to her obituary, Sarah, wife of Arizona guide Allen Doyle who accompanied Zane Grey in the early twentieth century, descended the Canyon and crossed the Colorado River in 1891 after Bright Angel Trail was completed.[2]

In 1893 author Sharlot Hall, the Arizona state historian, and a group of friends descended into the Canyon, returning to the rim after dark, thus becoming the first women to travel the trails at night.[3]

One of the earliest published accounts of a woman's visit to Grand Canyon appeared in 1891 as a series of newspaper articles by Virginia Dox. She traveled four and a half miles into the Canyon, though not entirely to the Colorado River, carrying at times a fourteen-month-old baby for an unnamed companion.[4] In 1890, five years after Mrs. Ayer's descent, a woman in the bottom of the canyon was still a rarity, so much so that when a member of Robert Brewster Stanton's railroad survey party spied the delicate bootprint of a woman near Diamond Creek, Stanton's diary recorded, "One of the men, I shall not give his name, fell down and kissed it."[5]

Ada Diefendorf Bass was the first white woman to raise a family at Grand Canyon. Boston Conservatory-trained, she married the proprietor of the Grand Canyon stage, William Wallace Bass, in 1894. The family lived on the South Rim, and Ada cared for the many summer guests who patronized her husband's establishment, Bass Camp. Cisterns a thousand feet below the rim furnished rainwater for laundry purposes. It seems certain there was little time left over to pursue her musical career.[6]

By 1895 Mrs. J. Wilbur Thurber, wife of the Grand Canyon stage's "gentlemanly driver," also raised her family, at least part-time during the tourist season, on the rim when her husband purchased Hance's Grand Canyon Hotel. This was the camp where the Hollenback sisters stayed in 1897. The scarcity of water on the South Rim for the simple necessities of life created an even greater dilemma for these early housewives who entertained tourists. The insatiable demand for water by the tourists, who began to arrive in mass after 1905, conflicted with the centuries-old Indian concept of water and its conservative use.

Grand Canyon historians tend to overlook the moccasin-footed Anasazi woman who left no visible print on the earth as she silently descended into the Canyon to the *sipapu*, symbolic place of emergence of all people. For the Indian, the journey to Grand Canyon has always been a pilgrimage of the spirit. Minna Hollenback also regarded it as such because she returned time and again during her life to renew that first encounter she found so indescribable in her letters. Although the Canyon became one of the great passions of Minna's life, in later years she also came to love and befriend the Pueblo Indians along the Rio Grande, who spoke of her in hushed tones and called her a "queen," but more often, "Mother." Since she never married or had a family of her own, she probably cherished the term even more.[7]

Both Minna and Jo shared another kind of parental affection and that was for their dapper father, John Welles Hollenback, who made all material things possible. While in Arizona, Jo wrote to her seventy-year-old father, hoping she might again entice him to travel westward; they had gone to Mexico together earlier that year.

*In Camp
Grand Cañon of the
Colorado, Arizona
June 27, 1897*

As we sat out on our favorite point on the rocks at sunset last night, and gazed on the grandeur of that wonderful view beneath us, we both felt that we could not be as sorry as we might be to leave it all, if we did not both have the hope that we may see it again some time, for as Minna said there, "We hope to do some more travelling in our lifetime, and why couldn't some of it bring us here again?"

Then we both feel that we shall have the double incentive of acting as "guides" to the rest of the family perhaps, but whether we see it again ourselves or not, we certainly hope that you, one and all at home, may not fail to do so, and that before long too. Five days of comparatively easy traveling would bring you here to the door of the log house in which I am writing, and that kind of a dwelling would take you, you know, back to the days of your boyhood!

The first four days on the cars with the break of changing trains at Chicago, would not seem much, I should think, to those of us who have had a month of train life, at least two weeks at a time, in Mexico, and the only tiring part might be the stage ride from Flagstaff here, but even that by means of a camping outfit for one night might be broken by a stay at Cedar Ranch. Anyway, Minna and I have quite concluded even if one didn't take the trail trip to the river and back (as some don't who come here), a view of the Grand Cañon from the point where we were last night, and those from Moran and Bissell [Zuni] Points, easily reached by trail along the rim (with no "up and down" nor "zigzag" at all, if not wished), such sights might well repay one for coming many more miles than we have travelled to see them. And if the climate here should agree with all of you, as it has with us, and seems to with all who live at the Camp, you couldn't ask for anything more in the way of health.

As soon as your letters arrived, we carried them in all haste up to our favorite seat on the rocks overlooking the Cañon to read them there, where we have read most of our "home letters," for we love to have them associated with our favorite spot here, and how we wished as we were reading them that you all could be looking at "the grandest sight on earth," right before us!

We both want to thank you and Mamma so much for being so willing for us "to see all we can," when we feel that we have seen so much more than we have deserved already.

We will be sorry to be away from you all and Glen Summit that much longer, but if we can go to Walpi for that very curious sight [the Snake Dance], now that we are almost "on the spot," when compared to the distance it is from home, I think it will repay us, for we feel a good deal about it as one might about any curious custom which may soon figure only in history. That the chance we may have now may never come again, for these Pueblo Indians are fast becoming, as has been expressed, "booted and linen-collared citizens of Arizona," and their quaint and curious customs, so interesting to the white spectator, are rapidly dying a natural death.

We may be excused for "coming so far to see snakes," however, when I mention that we haven't met one wiggler yet, in spite of our rambles in the Arizona forests, so we really ought to see a few before coming home, just to remind us of our tramps in the woods of Glen Summit. However, we may not be able to make our plans hold for the snake dance after all, so you may see us home some time in July as planned at first. . . .

As for the Petrified Forest, in Chalcedony Park, we find that "our royal progress" in that direction has been already heralded before us, for last night we heard that Mr. Tolfree, the proprietor of the New Bank Hotel at Flagstaff, had received word from Mr. [Adam] Hanna inquiring when the Misses Hollenback would visit the Petrified Forest. Mr. Hanna is the one with whom we will make arrangements for seeing the forest from Adamana, a little station near Holbrook, on the Atlantic and Pacific R.R., but how the gentleman knew that we were even thinking of coming there, or even of our existence in fact, we cannot tell, as we haven't written to him yet, not knowing our plans ahead definitely enough for that, as that part of our trip would have to come after the nine or ten days camping tour to the Natural Bridge.

We shall not be surprised at any time now to receive an invitation from Mr. [Myron H.] McCord himself, the Governor of the Territory, to dine with him at his home in Phoenix, we are getting to be of so much importance evidently to the citizens in general! It is very pleasant to feel of so much importance, and to find so many people interested in your welfare, but as Minna said yesterday, "Everyone has done so much for us and have helped us in so many ways, that they have hardly left us a chance to exercise our American independence."

Tomorrow we go for our last horseback ride along the rim, and shall probably visit Bissell Point again, where one of the grandest views of the Cañon is to be had. Mr. Hance is also going to point out to us the site of his old trail to the river, as far as we can see it from here. That interesting individual has just been in the log house sitting-room explaining to four of us his interests in the copper and asbestos mines of the Cañon, of which there are fifty-eight! This is no "fish story," if it did come from the old Captain. He has four partners and the five of them have to work out $5,800 worth of claims every year, being the Government mining law, or one of them, that they must work $100 worth on each mine every year, in order to keep their claims. The mines, both of asbestos and copper, are very rich. He has promised us some samples from each of the two kinds of mines when we visit his log cabin on the rim tomorrow. When old John Hance starts to tell you the truth, he is very exact about it ("sure thing!"), and as all four of us were seeking exact information this evening, we learned many interesting facts about the mineral deposits of the Cañon, and many other things as well, for no one could be better informed about this wonderful region than he.[8]

Minna inserted a folded note in one letter to her parents during the summer; marked "PRIVATE" in very large letters, it was obviously intended for her mother's scrutiny alone. Although a young Victorian woman rarely discussed feminine health in her diaries and letters, as we shall see, that was not the problem after all.

> *New Bank Hotel*
> *Flagstaff, Arizona*
> *[undated]*
>
> We are both well. I was afraid that seeing a note marked "private," you might think it was to ask advice about our health; but our different organs are working regularly and this is for something much less important.
> Louise wrote me that "your mother gave us your letters to read" and Papa said that our "letters were much enjoyed by the Hollenbacks, Haddocks, Athertons, Bixbys, Taylors, etc." [family and friends] Now all these compliments are much appreciated, and I suppose the Hollenbacks might enjoy any news from their absent members, but I don't think my scribbles are worthy a place in a circulating library. Of course I do not mind *most* of them being seen by the *immediate* family (H-s & T-s) [Hollenbacks and Twyefforts], the Haddocks, or possibly Louise [?] if she is in our house at the time;

but to think of that doubtful privilege being accorded to the third and fourth generation is an absolute clog to one's pen, and don't, oh, don't, send them to the Athertons! Please don't think me entirely a crank if that thought freezes my ink and paralyzes my fingers. I simply *can't* write for an audience, and why should I?

At home, when we want to have a little conversation with one of the family, we are not obliged instead to deliver a lecture before the assembled family of our intimate friends; and to be forced to that, just because we are far from home, seems a little hard. When dead ink and paper are the only substitutes for living sight and precious "talks," there is no great selfishness in wishing that one means of intercourse to be as free as possible, that we may speak from our hearts if so moved, without fear of the eyes of even the nearest outsider.

I understand well enough that there may have been times when you couldn't get out of it, or that the practice may not have been so general as it sounded, —but if it was, and if it should go on, I would dread home letter writing only less than school essays. That is unnatural, and seems to me unnecessary. If I have misunderstood the allusions referred to, forgive me; and if you think me unreasonable, tell me so when we get home, but *keep all letters with any sentiment in them to yourself, and don't give the others to anyone but Hollenbacks, Taylors, Beards, Haddocks and Cousin Em (if she visits you)* and *please be careful what you give to them.* That is a pretty liberal allowance. Will you please make the rest of the family understand all this? Jo has been writing Nan to the same effect. We don't want to restrict ourselves to postal cards.

I enclose some scribbles, made long ago at the Cañon thinking they might amuse Juliette. . . .[9]

In New York City during early May 1897, Minna and Jo had attempted to arrange their Southwest trip itinerary so they might travel with a Princeton professor named William Libbey, Jr., and his group of easterners. But the departure date of the all-male entourage appeared uncertain (perhaps intentionally), so the eager sisters decided to leave earlier at their own convenience.

A history-making event would occur on June 30, 1897, without Professor Libbey and his friends, when Minna, Jo, and John Hance would "punch the breeze" on the South Rim as they investigated a promontory at Grand Canyon that became known as Hollenback Point. In her letter Jo reiterates the date, June 30, as if to firmly establish it in the pages of Grand Canyon history. Even so, the name Hollenback Point would be forgotten for most of the twentieth century.

New Bank Hotel
Flagstaff, Arizona
July 2, 1897

. . . we have already done something, although the N.Y. papers haven't yet made mention of it—and now I have come to the best news of all. . . . To be sure we did not make the "discovery" entirely by ourselves, but like Prof. Libbey's, all well-ordered expeditions have to have an experienced leader, and ours in this case proved to be the noted Capt. John Hance, with whom I trust, you all feel sufficiently well acquainted already, so that he needs no further introduction. It might be well, however, to emphasize in passing, what we have already told you, I think, about old John's ability to tell you the "whole truth and nothing but the truth" when he starts out to do so, in spite of his usual proclivity for stories as "tall" as the rocks of his beloved Grand Cañon. Otherwise you might be inclined to believe, as we were at the very first moment, that the Captain wasn't making the "discovery" for the first time with us, but there was no doubt about it after that first second's hesitation, and the old Captain's delight in it all was as great and genuine as our own.

It all happened on the thirtieth of June, last Wednesday, and our last day at the Grand Cañon. As we had already made all the tours of interest along the rim to which Mr. Hance could take us and come back to the camp in one day, and only two days before had been the first to go over the whole of his new trail, along the rim, to Point Moran . . . we became possessed with the desire to see a little more before we should leave on Thursday.

So he told us that there was one other point on the rim, beyond Bissell's Point, about twelve miles from camp, and he had taken very few there, but he considered the views very fine, and thought we could get some good photos. So we arranged to take the day on Wednesday, June 30th, to have an early start, ride to the place he mentioned, have our lunch there and stay a couple of hours perhaps, then back to camp in the afternoon. We didn't expect to make very good time, for after leaving Bissell Point, there was no longer any trail, and for six miles we would have to find our own, through the pine forests, stepping over fallen trees of smaller sizes, and dodging under branches of cedar trees. Mr. Hance went ahead and broke off many brittle branches of the latter, which otherwise might have given our faces a few crimson stripes to add to our war paint of tan.

Oh! Nan and Julie, how we did wish you were with us, it was

such fun, and after we got off the trail and had left Bissell Point behind us, the spirit of adventure seemed to be in the very air, but even then we didn't know what we had before us.

I was constantly hoping that we might, at least, meet a mountain sheep, the big horned variety, for Mr. Hance pointed out the tracks of one, before we had left the Moran trail, which showed so plainly in the dust, that it seemed that the shy animal couldn't have passed that way very long before us. Mr. Hance said afterwards that he thought he was keeping out of our way, for no doubt it would not take him long to hear the tread of three horses' hoofs, and Minna could tell you that her "Sabine's" lovely song, a mixture of a groan and a grunt, with a wheezing intonation added, might have served to give some slight warning of our approach.[10]

We had gone on this way, in single file, sometimes keeping near the rim, where we had every once in a while the grandest views of the Cañon, then having to leave it to find a better path, more inland through the forests, for some three miles beyond Bissell Point, when gradually the innocent looking clouds of the morning grew blacker and blacker and it began to rain in good earnest. This didn't worry us, as we had expected as much when we left the camp, for the rainy season begins about July 1st at the Cañon, and it rains some nearly every day, but the showers are short and serve to settle the dust.

We were just then near the rim of the Cañon, at a magnificent point for a view, and we thought we would go a little farther down and then leave our horses and hunt for some shelter among the rocks, which are often very easy to find, for although the shower might be short we didn't intend to take any more of it than we could help.

Just as we were leaving our horses, Mr. Hance exclaimed, "It looks very much as if there were some cliff-dwellings over on that point." Sure enough it did, and it looked as if we might easily reach them too. So we hurried on, out onto the point some seven hundred feet and began climbing up the rocky hill in front of us, the very summit of the point, which stretched out into the Cañon with awful precipices surrounding it on all sides, except where a sort of saddle of rocky land about ten feet wide connected it with the main rim, and over which we had come.

On we hurried, the rain almost forgotten in our eagerness to reach the top. Mr. Hance, as excited as we were, skipped from rock to rock like a most animated chamois, and we soon saw that the surroundings were as new to him as they were to us. When we finally reached the top we discovered the ruins of what must have been a five or six roomed cliff-dwelling, the best preserved Captain Hance admitted, of any of the ruins which he knows anything about at the Cañon. One of its fort-like walls, right on the edge of the precipice, still stands as high as my head, and even those which have tumbled have more the appearance of having come to grief by means of erosion than by willful destruction by the hands of men. Then there was nothing anywhere to indicate that anyone else had been there before us, if so it couldn't have been for many years or Captain Hance would have heard of it. But he, who is better acquainted with the Grand Cañon than anyone else in the country, wasn't even aware that there were any ruins of cliff-dwellings on that point, where until that day he had never stopped himself, although, as he told us, he had many times gone by on his way up the Cañon. But it had always been farther inland on the main rim, through the pine and cedar forest, so that he had never been near enough to discover them before.

Soon after, it stopped raining, and Mr. Hance went back to our horses for our cameras and the lunch, for our new discovery proved so interesting that we decided then and there to eat our luncheon in its ancestral kitchen, or the spot, surrounded by its tumbled walls, which we imagined to be those of the kitchen of its cliff-dwelling owners.

Without even trying hardly, we picked up broken pieces of five or six different kinds of pottery; besides one small flint arrowhead and a piece of a light blue stone about this size which the jeweller here thinks may be the light blue, cheaper variety of turquoise.

The precipices right down from this ancient, fort-like dwelling, looked in some places to be fully 2,000 feet. Mr. Hance was actually scared at the sight in some places, and called it, "awful, sure thing!" To think of human beings ever dwelling in such a place in any degree of safety, especially to little children, seems almost incredible.

We took several pictures of the point, the last one in my large camera being devoted to the point to that side where the highest wall of this ancient little fortress showed to the best advantage, with Captain Hance standing down at the foot of the wall and Minna up on some of its ruins.

When we reached camp that evening, we heard Captain Hance describing the new discovery to the various domestics at the log house, giving the finishing touches perhaps to what we had already told Mrs. Thurber as soon as we came home. She was very much interested in it and said the place, as a point of interest, ought to be named. Later in the evening, Captain Hance and Mr. Clayton, the "general manager," came into the log house sitting-room and said that they had named the discovery "Fort Hollenback!"[11]

Think of that my dear family, so that now when your turn comes to visit the Grand Cañon, one of the points of interest which you will be urged to visit will be this very little "fortress" which bears your own name, for the old Captain says that he intends to build a trail out to it, but as no one will be likely to go out there unless he acts as their guide, he is going to see to it that not a stone is removed from its place, but that all care possible is taken to preserve it, as well as one of those queer little "stone houses," which the cliff-dwellers used to build under the ledges of overhanging rock, a very good specimen of which we also discovered there.[12]

I am so sorry that this just missed the ten o'clock mail yesterday, so I want to add now Minna's and my thanks to Mama for the delightful box of fire-crackers [candy] which arrived yesterday, and which we are enjoying so much. They are quite a source of wonder here. Mrs. Knox thought they were real.

We are both "very well and happy. . . ."[13]

Minna wrote to thank their parents for their patience and generosity. The sisters never took for granted the ability to travel worldwide, made possible by parental money. Whenever traveling, they kept expense records, Minna noting who owed whom and what amount. In fact, it was frugal Minna who became the Hollenback family's financial manager after her father's death in 1923.

Grand Cañon Camp,
Arizona
[undated]

"Only a few lines" to thank you for that most comforting and reassuring letter. First for the letter itself and then for the full and generous help from both you and Papa that has quieted our consciences and made the fulfilling of our plans seem so sure and easy. For we did feel cheeky to be asking for more time and still more so when it came to asking for money, though we knew you would understand and sympathize. But now we only have to thank Papa for his liberal kindness and you for making us feel that you were glad to have us stay and not consenting only that we might not be disappointed; then we can give three cheers and be happy. It is a great thing to have one's home people so interested that they actually seem to be travelling with us.

We have fallen into the habit of taking all our letters up to the rocks to read, for we have not missed an evening on the rocks yet and the stage comes in just before sunset. Jo says she feels as if you must all have been there, you have talked to us so often in that same place. On those rocks we have sat and talked, joked with other people, eaten chocolate, taken pictures, given yards of information to new arrivals, or more often only sat and thought and looked while night after night the colors changed to new beauty and the Cañon grew from an awful forbidding realm of another planet to a kind of protecting presence, grander and more beautiful but no longer oppressive. Sometimes I think that a person might feel safer here than in any other place on earth. It seems too calm, too great for any of the harms and bothers that vex the outside world to live near the shining of its walls. And it is in such a place that we have laughed and grown warm and friendly toward all the world over the dear home news, and there we have shaken hands and congratulated each other because some day we may be able to lead the family up there and then just sit to one side and jubilate over their happiness. But we won't talk to you. On our first view of the Cañon, two kindly intentioned tourists went up with us and asked us what we thought of it and if it wasn't grand. You will excuse me if I keep a little wondering pity for those misguided individuals.

I meant to have told you that Papa need not send the money until we sent for it, as our stay—and consequently our need—is still doubtful. But if he has already sent it we will take good care to bring back all that is unused. We are not so very confident about our being able to go to the Snake Dance, as we have not heard positively that any one is going except men. But several ladies have expressed a desire to see it, and if they think of going sometime perhaps they will be glad to take the time when two other women (that makes me feel old!) want to go also. Anyhow, we are going to try to stir up the population of Flagstaff, and as they are both enthusiastic over Arizona wonders and very hospitable to tourists, we may succeed very well. Or if we don't we may still be able to join a party from some other place; at least we will leave no stone unturned. And if we fail, we will go back to our Glen Summit with a sense of having done what we could. We wrote to you so hurriedly because we could say or do nothing until we had your consent, and we want the matter settled because it makes a difference in the order of our itinerary.

Flagstaff, July 5

All this was written a week or two ago, and if it is a little chestnutty please excuse it, for I don't like to think of that time as wasted.

I was happily mistaken about the Snake Dance. It now seems as if we were going "sure thing," for people are already arranging for the trip and there is no longer any practical doubt of our being able to get there. Instead, the only trip that seems somewhat misty is the one we thought the surest,—that to Montezuma's Well and Castle. Most Flagstaffians have been there already and the rest seem to be saving up for the Snake Dance, so I am afraid we shall have to depend on chance tourists. We can't go alone because it means a week or more of camping, and this is the only occasion we have had for wishing ourselves men. Indeed it is surprising how much a girl can do alone in this country, and how comfortably she could take a horse and be off alone all day with no fear of unpleasantness. The very stage drivers are a kind of mixture of reverential respect and fatherly kindness and the roughest-looking crowds are no harder to encounter than one's friends at an afternoon tea.

The people you meet have known you for about five years, apparently, but they are not pushing. Oh no. Perhaps all this results from social equality. Your chambermaid is as quietly respectful as an English servant, but she goes to classical concerts with the Observatory professors and you may find one of your "upper crust" friends taking a position as a hotel waitress. I must say I like it.

Tell Nan that this is the place for her to try her experiment; they are looking for a chambermaid at the Grand Cañon. She would be one of "the family" and could send her wages to the Junior Republic.[14] Besides, Capt. Hance said that whenever any of our family should come to the Cañon the best horses and the best saddles would be waiting for them, and that he would take them wherever they liked whether anyone else wanted him or not. There's a prospect for her!

Perhaps this view of things is only the result of an extra-pleasant experience, but our trip has certainly been more like a series of visits to families of cousins than anything else. As far as our knowledge goes, there seems to be no reason why a girl can't do as she likes, except those old conventionalities. When I am gray-haired and the conventions will let me alone, I hope to come out here and take all the camping trips I want without waiting for the uncertain company of possible tourists. As Jo says, anything we might do here would be less unpleasant than a shopping trip to New York, which justifies Mr. Lummis's assertion that we would "be safer here than in New York."

We are thinking of going to the Petrified Forest, Laguna and Acoma (one trip) next week. That will give the party which is trying to gather itself together for the Natural Bridge time to make up its mind. Mrs. Sisson can't go after all, and the arrangements—though I think sure,—are not moving with as lightning-like rapidity as we could wish. Also the busy season has but just commenced, and after the C. E. [Christian Endeavor] convention, there will probably be people here who want to go to the Well and Castle. Meanwhile we might as well improve our time. Thursday we are going up Sunset Mountain with Mrs. and Miss Knox, Mr. Corser and I don't know who else, and tonight (Tuesday) we are going to make another attempt to storm the Observatory [see Chapter 2]. Wish us better luck than last time. . . .

What do you think of your distinguished daughters? The idea of leaving our name on a piece of the Grand Cañon makes me feel rather small, though the name is about long enough to reach half way round the particular rock to which they have fastened it. I almost envy myself when I think of the fun we had "cork-screwing" (Jo's word) through the cedars, scratching between twisty piñons, picking our slow way over untrodden rocks, and each minute undecided whether to keep a lookout for branches or to trust to luck and look at the Cañon.

The horses don't take the trouble to avoid branches but they can be trusted to keep a good foot from the nearest yucca, and I for one cannot blame them. One day I unknowingly sat down on a yucca and "I'll never do so any more." I understand now why its relative is called the "Spanish bayonet."

July 10

This letter is going to be a curiosity when I am through with it. It is a written record of our somewhat mercurial hopes and fears, and after contradicting myself two or three times in three pages I am afraid that your only lasting impression will be that your children do not know their own minds and had better put themselves in charge of a responsible nurse. But good bye to "perhapses" and "maybes"! The next piece of news is real news that you can depend upon.

Next week, Wednesday if possible, we are going to start for the Natural Bridge, Montezuma's Well and Castle and any other places of interest that we may happen to meet on the way. It is a ten or more days' wagon trip, as genuine camping as any of us are likely to experience, and best of all, the driver is the only man in the party. After waiting around several days for something to turn up, we concluded that if anything did, we should have to do the turning, so we stirred up an agitation with the joyful result that Mrs. and Miss Knox, Mrs. Olney, Jo and I are going to shift for ourselves, there being absolutely no reason why we shouldn't. The other people concerned are Mr. Wilcox, the livery-stable keeper, who is to drive and take care of us, and his little girl whom we are to take care of as she has no one at home.

I will save the details for Juliette.[15]

The summer was quickly slipping away. With each passing day, Minna and Jo became more and more self-assured in their camping ventures. From their account of the Verde Valley venture, one can only wonder what the captive liveryman, Elias Wilcox, might have said after escorting the female campers among the desert centipedes, known in the Hollenback family circle as "pidies."[16]

The letters and photographs by Minna and Jo from Verde Valley, their next Arizona camping destination, are some of the earliest recorded by women tourists to Montezuma Well and Castle; 1897 was also a historic year to have traveled to these Indian cliff dwellings south of Flagstaff, for it marked the first conservation effort by Arizonans to protect ancient if misnamed ruins of monumental significance.

Notes

1. *Arizona Champion*, May 23, 1885. See also Lockwood, *Life of Edward E. Ayer*, 98–99. Ayer was the founder of the Ayer Lumber Co., in Coconino County, and also a founder of the Field Columbian Museum in Chicago. Though Ayer Point in Grand Canyon is named for Mrs. Ayer, the name was never formally approved by the U.S. Board on Geographic Names. Barnes, *Arizona Place Names*, 137; Orth to author, April 29, 1987. Edward Ayer's left foot was deformed, which undoubtedly made the Grand Canyon descent no easy task for him. John Hance, along with W. F. Hull and Silas Ruggles, first entered Grand Canyon on June 22, 1874. Hockderffer, *Flagstaff Whoa!*, 148.

2. "Interview with Bert Cameron, June 21, 1939," Grand Canyon Items, 2 (1886–1914), GCRL; *Flagstaff Coconino Sun*, May 11, 1923.

3. Hall, "How I Saw the Grand Canyon of the Colorado at Midnight," 724–27.

4. *Albuquerque Daily Citizen*, Aug. 26, 1891; unidentified newspaper clippings, HA, Albuquerque; Barnes, *Arizona Place Names*, 143; *New York Times*, Feb. 15, 1941; *Hartford Courant*, Feb. 15, 1941. In July 1892 Mary Smith noted in John Hance's Visitor's Book: "Our crowd, ladies and all, made trip from cabin to river, and back to cabin and up to head of trail in one day. According to Mr. Hance, 'beating the record made by ladies.'" John Hance's Visitor's Book, AHS. Dox Castle, in the vicinity of Shinumo Creek

west of present-day Grand Canyon Village, was named for Virginia Dox on June 3, 1908. Born in 1852 in Wilton, N.Y., she was also the first woman teacher on an American Indian reservation, living at Pawhuska Mission, Oklahoma, in 1885.

5. Stanton, *Down the Colorado*, 205.

6. Maurer, *Grand Canyon by Stage*, 2; Hughes, *In the House of Stone and Light*, 50. The Havasupai Indians called Bass Camp *A-ha-ka-che-wa-ke-che*, meaning "water pockets." See also Leavengood, *Grand Canyon Women*.

7. Interviews during 1980–1982 with Maria Martinez and Blue Corn Calabaza, well-known potters of San Ildefonso Pueblo, N.M., who often visited and stayed in Amelia's Santa Fe house during the 1930s and 1940s.

8. JH to father, June 27, 1897, HC. John Hance was the first to find asbestos in Grand Canyon. His mine was located across from Red Canyon, today called Asbestos Canyon. Forced to carry the ore across the Colorado River, Hance then packed it out on burros up Red Canyon Trail (New Hance Trail). Billingsley, "Prospector's Proving Ground," 74. Mining in Grand Canyon began in the 1870s at a silver lode found by Charles Spencer in Havasu Canyon. Soon after, unfounded rumors of gold spread. Although there were literally hundreds of claims in Grand Canyon, few prospectors survived to tell of their unsuccessful attempts. The Orphan uranium mine in 1951 proved to be the only valuable discovery. The value of a miner's land and trails as tourist facilities, if he had lingered in the area that long, would have eventually exceeded any profits gleaned from ore. The miner was required to "prove" his claim before being allowed to patent it. Because of the great difficulties of mining in the Canyon, many claims were simply abandoned, along with the burros, thus the beginning of the burro overpopulation in the twentieth century. Hughes, *In the House of Stone and Light*, 47, 111.

9. ABH to mother, marked "Private," undated note, HC.

10. According to Stephen Whitney (*Field Guide to the Grand Canyon*, plate 61), bighorn sheep are a rarity today near the Canyon rim.

11. The earliest published record of the name "Pt. Hollenbeck" [sic] appeared on a map from ca. 1904 of Grand Canyon (U.S. Patent, Aug. 21, 1900) in a booklet accompanying a set of stereoviews. *The Grand Cañon of Arizona through the Stereoscope* (1907), GCRL. In Higgins, *Titan of Chasms* (126), "Hollenbeck Pt." is mentioned in the text. A map in this same booklet records "Papago Pt. (Hollenbeck)." According to the U.S. Board on Geographic Names, Papago Point was approved on July 3, 1906, with no listing of Hollenback Point as a former name. Orth to author, April 29, 1987. A telephone conversation with Dr. Bernard Fontana (Oct. 19, 1984), noted Papago scholar at the University of Arizona, Tucson, revealed no sacred Papago mythology associated with Grand Canyon. With this information, the author then petitioned the U.S. Board on Geographic Names to allow Papago Point to revert to its original name (with corrected spelling): Hollenback Point. Author to Orth, Oct. 20, 1984. The request, also reviewed and approved by the Arizona State Geographic Names Board, was approved by the U.S. Board on July 11, 1985, with the official designation published in Decision List 8503. Pinkerton to author, June 12, 1985; Orth to author, July 25, 1985.

Hollenback Point: point of land, in Grand Canyon National Park, on the South Rim of the Grand Canyon, 5.6 km. (3.5 mi.) S.W. of Desert View; named Hollenback Point in 1897 by John Hance in honor of Amelia B. Hollenback and her sister Josephine W. Hollenback, visitors to the park in that year; Coconino Co., Arizona; 36 degrees 01'23" N, 111 degrees 53'06" W; 1906 decision revised. Not:

Hollenbeck Point, Papago Point (BGN 1906), Point Hollenbeck.

Hollenback Point, east of Zuni Point, is inaccessible to tourists today.

12. Captain Hance was instrumental in naming other points of interest in that part of the Canyon, places with which "Fort Hollenback" holds its own in terms of interest. He named Ayres [Ayer's] Peak for Mrs. Edward E. Ayer, the first woman who climbed the peak and also the first one Hance took down to the river. He named Point Moran when Thomas Moran was painting his noted picture there; Hance helped him carry his equipment to the point and afterwards built the trail for tourists.

The promontory known as Bissell Point was named for W. A. Bissell of San Francisco, general passenger and ticket agent for the Atlantic & Pacific Railroad; the naming ceremony took place at Grand Canyon in 1892. Bissell, Calif., was also named for him. *Flagstaff Coconino Sun*, June 9, 1892; Marshall, *Santa Fe: The Railroad That Built an Empire*, 353. Apparently, the correct spelling of the name is "Bissell," rather than "Bissel," as it appears in the records of Domestic Geographic Names, U.S. Board of Geographic Names. The archivist of the Santa Fe Railway Archives, KSHS, confirms the spelling. Menninger to author, July 21, 1994. By 1906 Bissell Point was called Zuni Point, as shown on a Santa Fe Railway map, but this same promontory became known as Comanche Point because of George Wharton James's book, *In and Around the Grand Canyon*. On page 87, James refers to "Comanche (Bissell) Point." His use of these names as the same promontory has been perpetuated ever since. See, for example, *University of Arizona Bulletin* No. 2, 6 (Jan. 1935); Barnes, *Arizona Place Names*, 141; and maps in *The Grand Cañon of Arizona through the Stereoscope*, GCRL, and Higgins, *Titan of Chasms*, 25.

13. JH to family, July 2 to 4, 1897, HC.

14. The purpose of the George Junior Republic, an institution founded in 1895 by William Reuben George near Freeville, N.Y., was to educate young people in the economic, civic, and social structure of self-government based on that of the United States. Problem and neglected boys and girls from the city, the average age sixteen years, spent the summer living in boarding houses, later in cottages, and learning citizenship.

15. ABH to mother, July undated to 5 and July 10, 1897, HC.

16. Elias Wilcox ran the Grand Canyon Stage (owned by the Atlantic & Pacific Railroad), which traveled from Flagstaff to the South Rim between 1892 and 1895. Madsen, "Grand Canyon Tourist Business of the W. W. Bass Family," 14–15.

"Mrs. Stevens's house." Fort Leavenworth, Kans.

"Ambulance and Yale, in front of the house." Fort Leavenworth, Kans.

"Starvation Point [Peak], from the train, at sunset." Near San Miguel del Vado, N. Mex.

"The natural bridge, Petrified Forest." Near Adamana, Ariz.

"San Francisco Mountains, from the back steps of the New Bank Hotel, Flagstaff."

"Thurber's Camp, Grand Cañon. June-July, 1897." Grand Canyon, Ariz.

"Waiting for judges' decision, Flagstaff [rodeo], July 4, 1897."

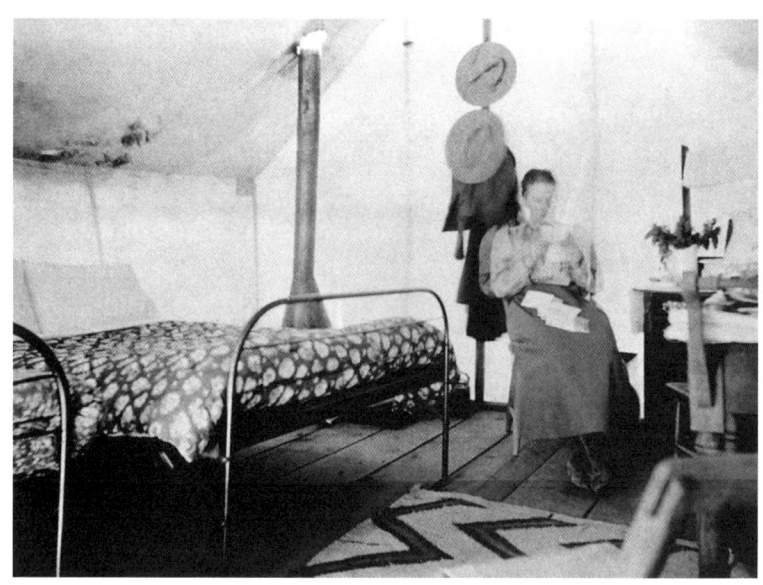

"Our tent." Thurber's Camp,
Grand Canyon, Ariz.

"John Hance." Early guide at
Grand Canyon, Ariz.

"John Hance's house,
by his old trail."
Grand Canyon, Ariz..

"Chums." Baby Grace Thurber. Grand Canyon, Ariz.

"Jo, Minna, Kitty and Fatty at the foot of the trail." Grand Canyon, Ariz.

"View toward camp from Bissell [Zuni] Point." Grand Canyon, Ariz.

"View down the Cañon, from Bissell [Zuni] Point." Grand Canyon, Ariz.

"Hance's Peak [Sinking Ship], from the rim trail." Grand Canyon, Ariz.

Amelia Hollenback at Grand Canyon, Ariz.

"The Colorado River, at the foot of the New [Hance] Trail. Looking upstream."
Grand Canyon, Ariz.

"On the old [Hance] trail."
Amelia Hollenback and Lotty
Thurber. Grand Canyon, Ariz.

"Group in cliff-dwelling."
Grand Canyon, Ariz.

"Ruined cliff-dwelling on top of pillar."
South Rim, Grand Canyon, Ariz.

"A house site, east of Bissell [Zuni] Point."
Grand Canyon, Ariz.

Amelia Hollenback and other tourists
at Grand Canyon, Ariz.

"The Cañon from the rim, near [Thurber's] Camp." Ayer Peak, Grand Canyon, Ariz.

"On the way." En route to Verde Valley, Ariz.

"Montezuma's Castle." Verde Valley, Ariz.

*"Solid comfort on a hot day. The Soda Spring."
Amelia is far right. Verde Valley, Ariz..*

"Montezuma's Well, from the top of the rim." Verde Valley, Ariz.

"A cliff-dwelling, Montezuma's Well." Verde Valley, Ariz.

"On the way to Acoma." Amelia Hollenback, Nathaniel Berkovitz, and driver John Davis en route to Acoma Pueblo, N. Mex.

"Katzimo, (the Mesa Encantada) from the north." En route to Acoma Pueblo, N. Mex.

"Acoma and her cliffs, from the northwest." Acoma Pueblo, N. Mex.

Josephine and Amelia Hollenback in front of Juana Valle [Acoma wife of Gov. Solomon Bibo] house. Acoma Pueblo, N. Mex. Photo by Adam Clark Vroman, Natural History Museum of Los Angeles, Calif., neg. no. V918 (774).

"*The church and part of the town, from the south.*" San Esteban Church, Acoma, N. Mex.

"*Houses in the middle street, Acoma. From the plaza.*"

"*Mr. Bibo's house.*"
*House owned by Juana Valle,
Acoma wife of Gov. Solomon Bibo.
Acoma, N. Mex.*

"The middle street from the east." Acoma, N. Mex.

Acoma Pueblo.

"Church buildings from the northeast." Acoma, N. Mex.

"A sheep corral at Acoma."
Acoma, N. Mex.

"The waterworks of Laguna, and Nathanael [sic] Bercovitz." Laguna, N. Mex.

"Mr. [Moses] Bercovitz's house, Laguna, and his family."
Laguna Pueblo, N. Mex.

"Laguna from the railroad."
Laguna, N. Mex.

"Zuñi, from Mr. Graham's roof." Waffle gardens (center), Zuni Pueblo, N. Mex.

"Lucero, governor of Zuñi. Aug. 9, '97. Sugar!" Zuni Pueblo, N. Mex.

"On the steps of the teachers' house. Zuñi, Aug. 9, '97." Unknown Indians; Douglas D. Graham, trader ; Fannie J. Denis, matron, and Ella P. Denis, asst. matron. Zuni Pueblo, N. Mex.

*Spectators at a Kâkokeshi dance,
Zuni Pueblo, N. Mex.*

*"Miss Emilie's house, from which
the pictures were taken."
Zuni Pueblo, N. Mex.*

*"The Kâka, before the
Kâyamashi's [sic] dance."
Zuni Pueblo, N. Mex.*

"Lunch on the desert, second day out." En route to Hopi, Ariz.

"Southwestern point of the red mesa." En route to Hopi, Ariz.

"Noon camp at Big Burro [Springs], third day out."
En route to Hopi, Ariz..

"Our Light Brigade climbing the trail to Walpi [Hopi, Ariz.] on their mounts."

"Our house below the gap in the mesa." Walpi, Hopi, Ariz.

"Before starting for the Snake Dance." (l-r) Amelia Hollenback, J. Wilbur Thurber, Frank C. Reid, Florence Olney, John Francis, Walker (?), Elias S. Wilcox. Approaching Walpi, Hopi, Ariz.

"Sichumovi." Chile drying on house, First Mesa, Hopi, Ariz.

"Plaza of Sichumovi." First Mesa, Hopi, Ariz..

"Two sisters, below Mishonginavi [sic]."
Second Mesa, Hopi, Ariz.

"Working up to Walpi." Climbing trail to First Mesa, Hopi, Ariz.

"Walpi, from the trail to Sichumovi." See path worn in rock. First Mesa, Hopi, Ariz.

"East street of Walpi (and our hostess)." First Mesa, Hopi, Ariz..

"Sweeping the Dance Court, morning of the Snake Dance."
(Center) Sacred Dance Rock; (right) kisi (altar). Walpi, Hopi, Ariz.

"Reserved for a large party, afternoon of the S[nake] D[ance]."
Hollenback party lodgings at Walpi, Hopi, Ariz.

*Walpi Snake Dance, 1897. Hopi, Ariz.
George Wharton James (with tripod and camera);
Heinrich R. Voth (beard and white straw hat);
Frederick Webb Hodge (glasses, white shirt,
and tie); and Amelia Hollenback.
Photo by Ben Wittick, MNM neg. no. 16192.*

*"Before the S[nake] D[ance]."
Hollenback party at Walpi. (l-r) Unknown Indian,
Elias S. Wilcox, Florence Olney, J. Wilbur Thurber,
unknown ; second row) Harry P. Corser,
Amelia Hollenback, John Francis;
Frank C. Reid (on ladder).*

*Amelia Hollenback
at foot of ladder, with camera.
Walpi Snake Dance, 1897.
Hopi, Ariz. MNM neg. no. 2532.*

*"Moqui maiden at the rear
[west side] of Walpi." Hairdo
signifies maiden of
marriagable age.*

*"On the platform with us.
Mr. [Ben] Wittick's camera."
Walpi.*

"South court of Walpi, from a covered passage."

CHAPTER FIVE

Montezuma Had a Well and Castle in Arizona?

THE PREHISTORIC PEOPLES thought to be the ancestors of today's southwestern Indians built a cliff dwelling in central Arizona's Verde Valley. Early nineteenth-century visitors to the region erroneously believed the nested "apartment house" had been built by the Aztecs for their emperor Montezuma, thus its name. But by A.D. 1400, a hundred years before the time of Montezuma, the cliff dwelling had already been abandoned, leaving little trace of its inhabitants, the Sinaguas ("without water" in Spanish).

Archaeologists called these people Sinaguas because they hypothesized they came from the arid areas to the north around A.D. 1100. Little remains of their culture other than the cliff dwellings. Only a clan symbol of a rectangle containing straight and zigzag lines and a circular snake maze incised on the wall of a first-floor room remain to depict an ancient mystery untold by the early inhabitants of Verde Valley.[1]

Montezuma Castle, as the cliff dwelling is now known, became one of the first national monuments in the United States through the Antiquities Act of 1906. Conservation efforts were first undertaken in 1897 by the Arizona Antiquarian Association at the suggestion of its vice-president, Frank C. Reid of Flagstaff, who would later accompany the Hollenback sisters to the Walpi Snake Dance. A lawyer and Presbyterian elder, Reid was also an "enthusiastic and energetic student of archaeology." The actual labor of restoring the Castle was accomplished by Dr. Joshua A. Miller, then president of the association and, for a time, the superintendent of the Arizona Territorial Hospital for the Insane in Prescott.[2]

Dr. Miller carefully recorded the dimensions and materials used by the Indians in constructing the cliff dwelling, as he found it in 1897. Consisting of five stories with twenty rooms and measuring forty-eight feet from top to bottom, the entire dwelling was made of stone and mud mortar mixed with limestone. The twelve-foot-high square tower in the center he found in a "tottering condition," its right corner collapsing from reckless excavations made by curio hunters. Openings in the outer rooms assured light and ventilation for the inhabitants.[3]

Of particular interest to Dr. Miller were the dwelling's floors. Minna Hollenback also found them unique, noting them in her journal that summer:

Floors of Montezuma's Castle
(copy of mem. [memo] made on same day as visiting "Castle," or day after, as a label for samples of small floor sticks & reeds.)
Montezuma's Castle, Sat., July 17, 1897
Floors of Cas. [Castle] are composed, first of large beams set in walls (logs abt. 10 ins. or more in diam. outside ends burnt off) often supported by = [equal] upright logs in room beneath; across these a solid layer of logs abt. 5 inc. [inches] thro', side by side; across these ditto of str. [straight] twigs abt. 1/2 in. or more thick, over these a layer of reeds & straw & over these a hard packed layer of stones & clay (or mud). Floor or roof having parapet (top floor) has another layer of sma. [small] logs over the twigs, then as usual. Am not quite but pretty sure that it was that floor.[4]

Dr. Miller's description agreed with Minna's observations, with the added information that the willow twigs were bound together with yucca fiber, tied with a square knot, and at equal distance so that the ties were in a perfect line from one side of the room to the other.

These primitive details remained vivid in Minna Hollenback's memory for thirty-five years, coming to fruition in 1932, when she built her adobe house in Santa Fe. She re-created a similar ceiling in the entry of the house, using centuries-old carved beams collected from Acoma Pueblo. With classic simplicity, Minna filled her massive adobe home with many such historic architectural elements. Her knowledge of Southwest architectural methods had been accumulated during her nineteenth- and early twentieth-century travels.[5]

Dr. Miller also recorded in 1897, "One will find objects that give an air of freshness, such as finger marks in the mortar, the new look about the cut surface of the wood, the floors, etc., that makes one feel almost acquainted with the builders of this wonderful place, and that it had not been long uninhabited by human beings. Then when we consider the great accumulation of debris, droppings from birds, rats, bats, etc., to the extent of two and a half to three feet in depth all over the floor, we realize that it must have been ages, centuries perhaps, in accumulating."[6]

Over 3,000 pounds of materials were used to stabilize the crumbling cliff dwelling in 1897; all had to be hoisted fifty feet up the sheer face of the cliff to the first-floor level. Iron rods an inch thick in twenty-foot lengths and longer were used to anchor the teetering rooms to the back of the cliff, while a temporary corrugated roof was installed over the center tower.

Dr. Miller assured the reader of his article in the *Antiquarian* that all danger of falling from the castle's "giddy height" (a total of one hundred feet) had been removed by the construction of "stairs" between stories. Minna's photographs reveal that by "stairs" he meant only ladders, as the Indians themselves had used centuries ago, pulling them up in case of danger.[7]

As Minna discovered—and related in a letter home (below)—danger lurked at the top of ladders as well, on the climb to the Castle. There were other hazards, real or imaginary. An army surgeon stationed at Fort Verde, Dr. Edgar A. Mearns, visited the Castle in 1884, which was then in a deplorable state of disintegration. Dr. Mearns published an article in *Popular Science Monthly* describing and illustrating in scholarly detail what he had found. He contended that only vague accounts of the cliff dwellings had previously filtered down from early French trappers and prospectors in Verde Valley. Ten years later, the *Flagstaff Coconino Sun* reported that Dr. Mearns, by then a scientist for the Smithsonian Institution, had been "overcome by the breath of a Gila monster."[8]

Not far from Montezuma Castle and Verde Valley, approximately seven miles north, is Montezuma Well, a limestone sinkhole thousands of years old fed by underground springs. The well is a sacred place for present-day Native Americans. Crystal-clear water flows from the fifty-five-foot-deep well through a fissure in the limestone down to the valley floor via fossilized acequias (irrigation ditches) dating from A.D. 600; they were built by prehistoric inhabitants of the area. The valley is green (hence *verde*) and was once tilled by the Hohokam (Pima for "all gone") and Sinagua Indians. The Hohokams, the first permanent settlers in the Verde Valley, date to even earlier than the Sinaguas. They raised corn, beans, squash, and cotton and lived in one-room houses built on terraces at ground level near water and their fields.[9]

In 1897, before going to Verde Valley to see Montezuma Castle and Well, Minna and Jo traveled by wagon to even closer Sinagua ruins at Walnut Canyon, ten miles east of Flagstaff. Because these ruins were only a few yards from the old Flagstaff to Winslow wagon road, making them all too accessible for early pothunters, Walnut Canyon has been called a monument to vandalism. Minna and Jo visited the west end of the canyon near a place known as Fisher's Tanks, not a part of Walnut Canyon National Monument today. Here the four-hundred-foot stone walls made of fossilized sand dunes millions of years old resemble the cross-hatched markings of an ancient elephant hide. Farther east up the narrow canyon, eroded limestone walls provide a protected overhang for several hundred prehistoric one-room dwellings.[10]

To reach Verde Valley from Flagstaff in 1897, Minna and Jo Hollenback and their group of "all ladies, not counting the driver," followed a wagon road south to "the Verde," as it was called by the people of the area. Not far to the east was one of the possible sixteenth-century routes of the Spaniards Antonio de Espejo

(1583) and Marcos Farfán de los Godos (1598), as they traveled from Tusayan (Hopi) searching the Verde for the rich mines nearby. The Hollenback party traveled to the Verde by way of Woods Ranch, followed Rattlesnake Trail, and crossed Rattlesnake Canyon at Rattlesnake Tank.[11] They descended two thousand feet in altitude down a long, gentle slope. En route, both the sixteenth- and nineteenth-century traveler undoubtedly saw a few of the namesake reptiles of the area. From Rattlesnake Tank the route follows Big Dry Beaver Creek. Eventually, Big Dry Beaver joins Wet Beaver Creek, which waters and often floods the mammoth sycamores shading the foot of Montezuma Castle.

During the last two decades of the nineteenth century, Gray Horse Cavalry units beat a path through this area, blazing trees to clear a path on their way to Camp Verde (later called Fort Verde) and Fort Apache. The dry, hostile terrain matched the wily Apaches who had scavenged and plundered Spanish and other Indian travelers with impunity for centuries. Only the wild California mustang could survive on the scant forage, but its gray color made an all-too-visible target of the U.S. Army cavalrymen who rode them. Adna Romanza Chaffee, captain of the famous Gray Horse Troop, had extended his hospitality to Minna and Jo during their stay in Fort Leavenworth earlier in the summer, showing them his collection of Indian pottery and artifacts.

On the trip to Montezuma Castle and Well, Minna and Jo discovered the knack of Arizona desert camping and, most of all, the luxury of a refreshing plunge after a day of dusty travel. We can almost feel the moist relief they experienced as they buoyantly bathed in Soda Spring beside Wet Beaver Creek—with their clothes on, of course, modesty prevailing.

Though Montezuma's name echoes today in the Verde, in truth he never reached the area of his namesake monument nor, as Minna wrote to Juliette, experienced the "beneficent quicksand" beside a creek in a strange place called Arizona.

> *N.B. Not "New Banks Hotel"*
> *or "Hotel New Bank"*
> *Flagstaff, Arizona, Thursday,*
> *July 22, Finished Tuesday,*
> *July 27, 1897*

I started to write a letter to you from the Verde, but what with washing towels and drying dishes and watching the others do all the rest of the work, I didn't get beyond the sixth line. Oh for a picture that could show you your usually well, we'll say neat-looking sisters, as they appeared around that camp fire! And oh for a sight of Mr. Luey's [a Brooklyn tailor] face if he could see the work of his hands adorned with a liberal mixture of sardine-oil, candle drippings, wagon grease, fruit juice and Arizona dust, while its wearer peacefully slides down hills or crawls on all fours through caves. But don't harbor the idea that we lived entirely on dust. Oh no. We had fresh hot biscuits warranted to weigh three pounds apiece, ham and bacon and eggs and eggs and bacon and ham, and canned vegetables and preserves and "green corn."[12] The last two would have made even "salt pork and black bread" endurable. And Coffee! Poor child! Some day you will rub the sleep out of your eyes just as the treetops catch the first sunlight, and you will stumble over to where that big black steaming pot sits on its crackling pile, then you will just flop down anywhere on the ground with your tin cup full, fresh, fragrant, hot and delicious,—and you won't be ready to exchange it even for the tea table in our dear green room. Somehow, when anyone says "camp," that morning picture comes clearest to my mind. First, Mrs. Knox's cheerful voice coming from somewhere in dreamland: "Now I'll just start the fire and make some coffee," then the feeling of the cool morning air on one's face, a row of half-awake figures struggling out of their blankets and making sleepy jokes at each other's expense, the early stillness of the dark green trees and grayish sky, a stimulating scent of burning wood and fresh coffee, and Mrs. Knox's comfortable figure trotting about in a short skirt, voluminous apron and a capacious sunbonnet, a full half hour before the rest of us would have thought of picking up a stick of wood. Then suddenly there is a gleam of yellow light over your shoulder, the treetops turn golden green and the sky grows slowly bluer, and you turn around with a half-surprised "Why, there's the sun!" and a curious feeling that there is something impertinent about that self-confident ball, shooting inquisitive rays into our cool retreat so long before he is wanted. Great is the glory of the sunlight, but the sun also brings the noonday heat that makes you seek the shady side of the wagon and wonder how you ever stood that pile of blankets last-night.

Now I am going to begin at the beginning, in the proper way. Perhaps you do not yet know that all these remarks refer to our trip to the Verde, that is, Montezuma's Well and Castle. Both of these are situated on Beaver Creek, a tributary of the Verde River, and within the wide Verde Valley, which is hardly ever dignified by its whole title, but goes simply by. . ."the Verde."

I don't believe that you realize the real usefulness of a wagon. By day it is a whole Pullman train, chair-car, baggage car, dining car and even sleeping car; by night it serves as a two-story shelter from storm. There is always the inside of the wagon if the rain should be too lively outside, and Mr. Wilcox and Viola (our driver and his little girl) slept under our wagon each night.[13] They at least had a roof over their heads! And if you want a tent, prop up the wagon tongue, throw a wagon sheet over it and there you are. Our wagon was a rattling, ramshackle old thing that seemed to be bidding goodbye to the world at every turn of its wheels. It had three seats, each wide enough for three persons, and a boot behind, whereon reposed our cots and a bale of hay for the horses. (Hay is usually intended for horses, but I mentioned its use so you wouldn't think we took it for bedding.) And the amount of things that matter, the things were almost everywhere excepting on the roof. All our provisions, in big tin cans, pails and wooden boxes, tin dishes, pans and kettles, canteens, telescopes (the carrying, not the astronomical kind), everything was piled in the bottom of that wagon. Then our blankets were folded over the seats instead of cushions, left at home to economize room, each one's pillow was wrapped in her shawl and laid against the back of her seat, and then we squeezed ourselves into whatever room was left. Of course, nobody minds curling up in a graceful Turkish attitude on top of the assembled baggage, or staying there most of the day; but when one of one's dainty Arizona shoes (about the size and thickness of a rubber boot) goes crashing through a pasteboard cracker-box while the other tries to overturn a jar of preserves, there is apt to be a mild feeling of rebellion.

I may camp out for months at a time somewhere in the coming years, but I don't think I shall ever forget that first night out, or think of it without laughing. We all had such different ideas of camping! We had imagined a nice shady place, ground strewn with pine needles, water somewhere near and the rustle of green branches over our heads. Instead, the water ran at the foot of a long hill that Mr. Wilcox didn't care to mount the first thing in the morning, when the horses would be stiff and might balk; so we went up and on till apparently we had grown tired of moving, then we just stopped and stayed where we were. It happened to be a great bare space edged around by the pine forest, a place left bare, one would think, because it was too rocky for anything to grow! Rocks were tumbled around too thickly to allow even foot-space between them, split and jagged, malpais fragments from the size of a watermelon downwards. We looked at our folded cots and were mighty thankful. Being still innocently impressed with a desire to do things properly and in order, we began to look around for a good "dining room," but poor Mrs. Knox, standing with a frying pan in one hand and a coffee pot in the other, grew tired of waiting for us and sat down triumphantly in the middle of the road! It was the only smooth spot for half a mile at least, so we followed her brilliant example, spread our oilcloth, set the table and sat down likewise. Later on, we abandoned all that ceremony. Real campers, in this country at least, don't bother to put things carefully in rows. The tin dishes are in a pile, the pots and kettles by the fire; you pick out your dishes, help yourself to whatever you want and sit down somewhere in peace and contentment. It is wonderful what an amount of useless fussing there is in the world. Do you remember how we used to envy the birds because all they had to do at night was to poke their noses under their wings? The camp process of going to bed is nearly as simple. It consists chiefly in taking off one's shoes and rolling into a blanket. After our first dishwashing we set up our five cots in a row and went to bed. It was barely dark, so of course we sat and talked, an operation that we kept up intermittently till sunrise. Mrs. Knox slept (she has a business-like way of doing whatever she sets out to do), the rest of us admired the view and sat up at intervals to tell each other about it, all night. Imagine it if you can. You are in bed, overhead there is nothing but clear dark space and countless stars and the slow moon that scarcely moves across; around you only moonlight and rough ground, mottled with rocky shadows, an occasional dark, lonely pine and the sound of the cattle calling to each other across the range. Not the mild "moo" of our gentle barnyard friends, but a kind of wild bellowing and shrieking and grunting that is a little disconcerting when one is not in the mood for grand opera. Once a band of horses came trotting along the road on their way to the creek. Evidently they didn't like our looks (we appeared to be a combination hospital ward and stable), for they stopped a few rods away, trotted first to one side and then to the other, gave several loud disapproving snorts and politely intimated that we were to get out of the way and let them pass! One white horse, whose coat gleamed finely in the moonlight, was especially active, but finding us deaf to their hints they finally made a wide half-circle into the woods and so went around us. That was the only amusement we had, except the chorus of what Jo calls "Arizona humming birds"; gazing sociably at each other, and killing mosquitoes. (It was we who indulged in these highly exciting occupations, not the bulls!)

 Next afternoon we reached Mr. Finney's [*sic*] bank on Beaver Creek, and there we camped for four nights. It takes such a little green to make an impression in this desert surrounded country! The first view of the Verde makes one wonder where it got its name. All you see is a wide sand-and-rock valley, filled with little flat-topped mesas, cut by dry watercourses and dotted with mesquite, greasewood, cacti and other thorny and ill-natured plants. Far away is one little bright spot, greener than anything we have seen this side of eastern Kansas. (Except the parrot that lives next door to Mrs. Olney, and greets me with "How do you do, Polly," in a sweet soprano voice.) It is an alfalfa field. But when you come to Beaver Creek you will no longer wonder at the name, narrow though the green strip is that divides the desert at its sides. For the creek runs jumping over the big stones, rejoicing, one would think, at the good it does; and its banks are arched over with stately sycamores and cottonwoods and hidden by tangled underbrush and wild grape vines, and the water ripples through tiny ditches across the orchards and fields till the place seems a little bit of the green East set into the arid landscape. Montezuma's Well is about half a mile down the creek from Mr. Finney's house.[14] Walking along the creek, there is no suggestion of anything unusual nearby, unless it is the fine cliffs on the right hand side. They are only 80 or 90 feet high, but imposing enough for all that, with their water-worn faces and occasional cliff dwellings. But who would think that all this solidity was a thin and hollow sham? That massive rock is nothing but old Monty's well curb (it is a pity that he never saw the wonders that are known far and wide by his name); in places it is scarcely more than five yards wide at the top, and in one spot it is hollowed out into a large cave whose walled mouth opens at the bottom of the well. Yet its face is as the foundation of a mountain, only at one place a clear strong stream rushes out of the rock, taking one by complete surprise. That is the outlet of the well. You climb to the top of the cliffs and there drops before you the big, round, cliff-walled hole with the still, mysterious pool at the bottom. A strange spring, truly! On the rim above the outlet are the walls of a ruined Pueblo, and the caves, once inhabited, are under this. But you probably know as much about the Well as I do, so I won't waste any more time in description. Wait till I get home!

What do you suppose Mrs. Knox brought home as a souvenir of the Castle? I know you'll guess it. Yes, it was a tarantula! A large, black, furry, fierce-looking spider, but fortunately it was dead when she found it. I was climbing serenely up one of the long ladders to Montezuma's Castle when I heard Mrs. Olney, on the ledge just above me, say to Mrs. Knox: "Didn't you see that tarantula?" "Where?" "Right by the head of the ladder." Imagine my feelings, next time you quake at the sight of an innocent "pidie"on your ceiling! Holding on to a ladder in mid air, so it seemed, with a wicked "fierce bug" sure to jump at me the minute my head showed above the next ledge! I was scared enough till I heard it was dead.

Bless the people who saved Montezuma's Castle. Excepting the Cañon, we have seen nothing that could ever impress a person as it does, from the time he first sees it standing, gray and lonely, in its cave, half way up the cliff, till he stands on its top-most platform looking through the neatly plastered little arrow holes that are so carefully slanted at exactly the right angle to reach any foe who might have won his way to the next lower story. What astonished me most was the solidity and neatness of the builders' work; I had supposed that such places were much more roughly put together. The building is five stories high, far more solid than the white, plaster-like rock about it, and its walls are smoother than the new American work that has been put in to preserve them. Descriptions and information may be had on application when we get home. I haven't enough of the latter in stock to bore anyone.

But the fun of the whole expedition was in the Soda Spring! It is just an ordinary-looking spring, exactly like one of our springs except that its sand is brown instead of white. But I have to thank that spring for the best song-and-dance ever seen outside of a comic opera. If you had only heard Jo squeal! The thing to do is to take a bath in the spring. After splashing around in the nice cool water, you decide that there is more room on the other side and you start across, but you don't get there! Such good walking as it is on that firm, level floor of smooth, sand, slump! There is nothing under you! You are going down to China! One squeal of terror and—pop! you are shot up into America again. I never felt such a queer sensation in all my life. Where the water boils up is a peculiar but kindly and beneficent quicksand, that instead of pulling people down buoys them up so that they can't sink! Sometimes one man stands on the shoulders of another and tries to push him down, but no, his head will stay up. Push a long pole downward with all your force, and the minute you let go, out it pops. It is something of an experience, this standing upright in water up to one's shoulders and frisking around, apparently on nothing at all. And the funniest part of it is walking across that shallow spring, then that horrible bottomless feeling, and working so hard to keep yourself down. No one knows how deep it is, so far as we heard. I wonder if our springs are like that?[15]

Minna jotted a postcard to her family about their camping trip to Montezuma Well and Castle. It would seem that poor old Mr. Wilcox had his hands more than full.

Flagstaff, July 22, 1897

This is in the nature of a telegram to let the family know that we are "well and happy." We returned here Tuesday afternoon from our record-breaking camping trip to M.'s Well and Castle. Camping is the greatest fun on earth! We broke the record by being, I think, the first party composed exclusively of ladies (the driver doesn't count) and by not having any quarrels! But we didn't break anything else worth mentioning.

It was not a hard trip, and Jo and I stood it better than any of the others. We will not be quite happy till we are started again. For the last day or so we have been so busy hustling for information about our next plans that we have not had time even to catch the home mail with a postal. Jo has heard from Prof. L. [Libbey]. He wants to go to the Snake Dance. We think it exceedingly kind of both him and Mr. Atherton to use time and trouble for us.

Oh dear! There goes the train! It is very nice to have a mail every day, but there are some inconveniences about having only a mail every day. I am writing to Julie . . . Oh, don't ever expect me to be enthusiastic over Huyler's candy when I might be reading letters![16]

The camping trip to the Verde gave the girls the added courage and stamina necessary for the approaching trek across the desert to the Hopi mesas and the Walpi Snake Dance. By the time the two sisters returned from Montezuma Castle and Well, Flagstaff was already bustling with activity in anticipation of the Indian ceremonial, which took place every two years on Hopi's most eastern mesa, First Mesa. The religious dance was intended to attract rain but instead drew people from across the United States. It also provided a money-making opportunity for the more industrious people of the area. Through the years it had become the social affair of the season. Though all were preparing, the Snake Dance was still three weeks away for the tourists. For the Indians, however, the religious ceremony would begin nine days earlier.

While the Hopis were making their sacred preparations, Minna and Jo boarded the one daily eastbound train to Laguna, New Mexico, to visit that pueblo and Acoma Pueblo to the south. The sisters earlier had caught only a fleeting glimpse of the centuries-old Laguna church from the train window on their way west to Flagstaff. They arrived in Acoma only a day after the ill-fated ascent on July 23, 1897, of Professor William Libbey, Jr. The Princeton professor was traveling to Acoma with Herbert L. Bridgeman, an explorer of note and business manager of the *Brooklyn Standard*, to ascend Katzimo, the Enchanted Mesa of Indian legend. Katzimo had always been a place of mystique whose legend was jealously guarded by Charles F. Lummis. At Acoma Minna discovered a strong sense of place in the remote Southwest, but Professor Libbey uncovered an archaeological hornets' nest.

Notes

1. The snake maze motif, an ancient, universal geometric form sometimes called a "Minoan Labyrinth" or "Troy Town," is a petroglyph portraying a difficult access to or emergence from some important point. Wellmann, *North American Indian Rock Art*, 96. In 1764 Jesuit Father Juan Nentvig mentions that the Pima Indians described to him an entire house built in a maze of similar design on the Gila River; Nentvig related, "This seems more like a house of amusement than the residence of a grandee." Nentvig, *Rudo Ensayo*, 14.

2. Miller, "Montezuma Castle Repair Expedition," 1:225–28, History Manuscript File, MCNML. Dr. Miller, a founder of the University of Kansas City, Mo., in 1881, first came to the Southwest in 1888. In 1892 Miller served as the first president of the Arizona Medical Association. In 1901 he died suddenly on a train in Flagstaff en route to the Hopi Snake Dance. Quebbeman, *Medicine in Territorial Arizona*, 237, 287, 313, 359.

3. Miller, "Montezuma Castle Repair Expedition," 225–28.

4. ABH 1897 Journal, HC.

5. The late John Gaw Meem, well-known Southwest architect, told the author in 1972 that when Amelia first asked him to construct a similar ceiling in her Santa Fe house, he had never seen one quite like it but did as she requested. To improvise the "twigs" placed over the wood beams (with a layer of straw placed over it), Meem used small round pieces from an ordinary Mexican shipping crate such as may still be found today. Amelia also more than likely knew the early Grand Canyon architect Mary Jane Colter, chief architect and decorator for the Fred Harvey Company from 1902 to 1948. The author found in the Mary Jane Colter Collection, MNMPA, a vintage photograph of a large portal beam built into an old Bernalillo, New Mexico, house. This identical beam, with its carving and the year 1828, was incorporated into Amelia's Santa Fe home. In addition, the Hollenback floors were of the simulated-mud flooring originally used by Colter earlier in Hopi House at Grand Canyon. Still visible today in the Santa Fe house—though not in Hopi House due to the heavy foot traffic—the floor consisted of an ox-blood-colored mastic layered over concrete. Hopi House, designed in the style of a Hopi Indian dwelling, was built in 1905 to house the Fred Harvey Indian arts salesrooms. Grattan, *Mary Colter*, 14. Today, it is a federal offense to remove artifacts from a national monument, but this was not the case when Amelia was building her home.

6. Miller, "Montezuma Castle Repair Expedition," 225–28. The handprint, pressed into the mud plaster and often appearing on a fireplace, is a characteristic marking in Southwest adobe architecture because plastering is done by hand without a trowel. Indian women traditionally do the plastering.

7. A National Park Service trail sign to the Castle ruins states that Montezuma Castle was closed to the public in 1951; the cliff dwelling may be viewed today from ground level only.

8. Apparently, Mearns fainted, perhaps from fright; he recovered. Mearns, "Ancient Dwellings of the Rio Verde Valley," 745–63; *Flagstaff Coconino Sun*, Sept. 6, 1894.

9. Schroeder and Hastings, *Montezuma Castle National Monument*, 4, 26–31; *Montezuma Castle Trail Guide*, 14.

10. Walnut Canyon National Monument was established Nov. 30, 1915, and contains 2,249 acres.

11. Bartlett, "Notes upon the Routes of Espejo and Farfán," 21–36. Woods Ranch is near present-day Interstate 17.

12. Arizonans still consider green corn a delicacy. Today, the Hopis bake their corn in field ovens, holes dug in the ground.

13. In 1899 both Viola Wilcox and her brother died of croup. *Flagstaff Gem*, Mar. 9, 1899.

14. The Robert Finnie house, where Minna and Jo camped, remains today; from 1930 to 1964 it was known as the Soda Springs Dude Ranch. Interview with Paul M. Webb, Finnie's son-in-law, Sept. 10, 1985.

14. ABH to Juliette, July 22, 1897, HC.

16. ABH to Anna, July 22, 1897, HC.

Chapter Six
Oh, To Be an Acoma Cow

THE INDIAN PUEBLOS OF Laguna, Acoma, and Zuni, not far from the railroad tracks in western New Mexico Territory, were yet to be explored by the Hollenback sisters by midsummer of 1897. The eager girls made up for lost time by visiting all three of the pueblos both before and after the Hopi Snake Dance held in late August.

On August 7, 1897, Minna and Jo attended one of the several rain dances held each summer at Zuni, danced by the Good Kachinas, the *Kokokshi*.[1] On their return trip to Acoma in early September, they witnessed the Feast of San Estevan, the patron saint for whom the Acomas named their church. Of the three pueblos, Acoma would make the most lasting impression on romantic Minna. To reach Acoma the sisters got off the train at Laguna and to reach Zuni, at Gallup. Whether in Arizona or New Mexico, leaving the railroad meant "pulling freight" (carrying supplies in a wagon) to reach the pueblos.

En route to Flagstaff in June, Minna and Jo had seen Laguna Pueblo, sixty miles west of Albuquerque, from the train window. It had been an unbelievably close view. The train tracks came to within a mere fifty yards of the ancient pueblo's whitewashed church, whose ceiling was made of tinted, herringboned *latillas* (small branches laid over wood beams). In 1881 army Capt. John Gregory Bourke described the gleaming white Laguna church as "a beacon planted in the midst of a restless ocean of strife and angry passion," the words sounding much like those of a church hymn. The train tracks came so close to Laguna, in fact, that Charles F. Lummis called the Laguna station "a parasite upon the picturesque Pueblo." Lummis lamented, as he often did, the fact that the young of that pueblo brandished all-too-American mannerisms and education. That, too, had arrived with the nineteenth-century hymn-singing missionaries.[2]

The tracks of the Atlantic & Pacific Railroad (by 1897 known as the Santa Fe Pacific) followed the route of the historic Santa Fe Trail from Fort Leavenworth, Kansas, over the precipitous pass from Colorado into Raton, Las Vegas, and Glorieta, New Mexico Territory. The tracks, however, never actually reached the city of Santa Fe itself.[3]

As the train pushed into New Mexico in 1897, the sisters' interest was quickly stimulated by the changing scenery. Jo wrote to their father, recalling their previous trip together through the Southwest and perhaps hoping to inspire him with her vivid descriptions to take another.[4]

New Bank Hotel
Flagstaff, Arizona
June 10, 1897

The ride from Kansas City was a little shorter than we first expected, for we left Kansas City at 1:45 p.m. on Monday, but reached Flagstaff yesterday at 11.30 a.m., when according to the time-table made out for us at the Raymond office in New York we had not expected to arrive here until 3:35 p.m. yesterday. They told me in N.Y., however, that there had been some changes in the time tables of this road very recently, but that they couldn't tell me just what they were.

We were almost sorry to leave the good old train, for we had enjoyed our two days' trip very much. Of course the greater part of the ride through Kansas was at night, that is west from the center, but I have seen it so recently and I don't think Minna missed much, for towards evening on Monday, it began to be very bare and prairie-like, plenty of sagebrush, but the scattered railroad settlements still too American like and unpicturesque to be very interesting. But by the time we were awake Tuesday morning, we were already in Colorado, and from there on the ride was one of great interest until we arrived here.

We took our breakfast that morning at the little town of La Junta, Colo., from which across the plains we had a lovely view of the beautiful Spanish Peaks. I little thought when we saw them last when we were together that I should see them so soon again! They say that Pike's Peak is at times visible from La Junta away to the northwest, but it wasn't that morning, for although clear it wasn't quite clear enough for that.

At La Junta we had our first experience of a Western railroad eating station, on this trip at least, for west of Kansas City there was no dining car attached to this train, but twenty-five minutes were given at the eating stations, and we found the food very good indeed . . . After leaving La Junta, we had beautiful views of the snow capped mountains until well on into New Mexico, and there we lost sight of them behind the towering heights of nearer mountains, of that spur of the Rockies which extends south to Santa Fe.

On our way to Raton, New Mexico, where we stopped for dinner, we were entertained by the antics of the fat, round prairie-dogs of which we saw great numbers close to the train tracks, and for the first time we saw one of those small prairie-owls, which are said to live in the same burrows with their four footed friends, calmly surveying the train with his little blinking eyes from the top of a prairie-pup's mound. He was not unlike his owl cousins of the East, though much smaller in size.[5]

On beyond Raton, more prairies followed which might have grown rather monotonous in spite of the sagebrush and prairie-dogs if it had not been that we were now approaching the land of adobe huts, which were at first curiously mixed, or combined, with the typical rude plank dwelling of the frontier ranchman, but farther south we passed whole villages of the adobe huts which reminded me strongly of Mexico, and gave us both visions of the curious Pueblo towns we hope to see. The owners of these huts, however, seemed to lack the attractive picturesqueness of the native farther South, for they looked in most cases like "poor whites," only occasionally we saw some who had the appearance of half-breeds, or Indians, and even they seemed too much of the north to indulge in the many-hued serape, but the Navajo blanket will soon take its place for us, I suppose, and that is certainly in most cases, brilliant enough to suit anyone.

Colonel Chaffee at the Fort [Leavenworth] had a beautiful one, which I wished Mamma could see. He had two in fact, but the first was of the kind that is nearly worth its weight in gold which only museums can afford to purchase. (This statement I fear must be qualified for although curious and valuable, it is the thinner kind which is the rarer and most expensive.) The Colonel had a very interesting little museum himself, in his back library, in his collection of Moqui and Navajo curios. Among his collection of pottery was one piece very much like the little jug and bowl you got me that night, you may remember, when the train stopped late in the evening at a little station in southern New Mexico; a kind very much unlike that made by any of the Mexican peons.

Right beyond Las Vegas, New Mexico, where we stopped for supper Tuesday night, we passed through the most lovely part of the mountain scenery, with open green valleys intervening; one which we went through, just at sunset, reminded us both very much of that lovely, peaceful Hayden Valley which you will remember we passed through in a carriage on our way from the Cañon to

Yellowstone Lake when we were in the Park.

Just as the sun was setting, a short thunder storm came up and for a few minutes the lovely valley was spanned by a rainbow which made nearly a complete arch, which we could see from the car window.

Not long before that we had been standing at the rear platform of our car, which was the last of the train, and Minna was able to take a photo of a towering isolated peak called "Starvation Mt." which we hope will come out good, though it was late in the day for very good results, but it was then or never.

"Starvation Mountain" was so named from the story which is told of it, that many years ago a company of ill-fated pioneers were captured by the Indians, and taken up there to conclude the terms for a treaty, but instead abandoned to starve to death, while the savages kept ground below. Whether true or not, the story adds interest to the frowning tower-like mountain, but unless those early settlers were very good climbers, I am inclined to think that the Indians must have carried them pick-a-back to have ever got them up there at all. . . .

Near the little station of Glorieta, New Mexico, we saw from the car windows and very near the tracks the ruins, still massive, of the old church of the Pueblo of the Pecos, built by the Spaniards 275 years ago, "before," as Mr. Lummis says, "there was a Saxon in New England."[6]

In his book, *The Spanish Pioneers*, which we bought in Kansas City and read on the train, he says that the Pueblo of Pecos was once the largest in New Mexico, but was deserted in 1840. Its great quadrangle of many storied Indian houses is in utter ruin, and unnoticeable from the train, but the ruins of the adobe church still remain and still make a very imposing pile of adobe brick. Going back I hope it will be earlier in the day so that we may get a snapshot of it from the train. . . .[7]

By the end of July, already half the summer had been spent amid the wonders of northern Arizona Territory. But from the moment Minna and Jo stepped off the train in New Mexico Territory, the Indian pueblos of Laguna, Acoma, and Zuni captivated them with their colorful history dating from the mid-sixteenth century. Like the Hopi mesas in Arizona, Acoma's high and inaccessible site lured all who saw it for hundreds of years, including Francisco Vásquez de Coronado and his army in 1540. Not all were explorers or tourists who came to conquer Acoma by way of one of its seven steep trails, where only coyotes prowled after dark. At least one visitor came to debunk an Indian legend.

The legend of Katzimo, known as Mesa Encantada (Enchanted Mesa) near Acoma Pueblo, as well as the origins of the Acoma people, is wrapped in mystery. The Acomas believe they once occupied an ancient village on top of this mesa. Evidence of farming, herding areas, and campsites in surrounding terrain seems to indicate inhabitation from at least A.D. 1200. As with all oral history, however, the knowledge of their history faded with the deaths of clans and their members.

The summer of 1897 marked not only the "Great American Trip" of the Hollenback sisters but also provided an episode in nineteenth-century history that a certain Professor William Libbey, Jr., of New Jersey would attempt to erase in his long career as a world explorer and lecturer. A professor of physical geography at Princeton and a world-famous rifle shot who had coached several U.S. Olympic rifle teams, Libbey set out to explore Katzimo, making a much heralded but laborious ascent of Katzimo on July 23 with the aid of ropes and a Lyle gun. It took him four days to assemble and properly aim the cannon shot with which to catapult a rope across the mesa to hoist himself up in a "bo'sun's-chair," equipment borrowed from the U.S. Life-Saving Service.

Professor Libbey told the *New York Times*, "My ascent of La Mesa Encantada . . . was made in exactly two minutes and forty seconds by the watch" (ignoring the several days of thwarted attempts). Much to his later regret, Libbey publicly released a hasty analysis of the top of the 350-foot-high Katzimo, finding "nothing that would indicate even a former visit by human beings." This careless analysis made immediate headlines. Public ridicule and condemnation by the relentless Charles F. Lummis and others followed in all the major newspapers across the United States. Conveniently, Lummis happened to be standing in the office of the *San Francisco Chronicle* on July 23, when Libbey's press release arrived. He unleashed the first of many volleys of verbal attacks that continued for months, even years, to come, declaring that "the most notorious and sensational confounding of a would-be scientist in the annals of American scholarship befell a college professor who 'spoofed' a tradition of the people of Acoma." The Katzimo incident no doubt caused untold humiliation for Professor Libbey. His ill-fated adventure on the mesa of "careless iconoclasm," according to Lummis, would be more or less forgotten by historians. Libbey probably hoped it would be forgotten forever.[8]

In September 1897 Frederick W. Hodge, from the Smithsonian Bureau of American Ethnology in Washington, D.C., quickly ascended Katzimo with only ropes and ladders (without incident, other than a sizable tear in his pants, as evidenced by photographs) in two and a quarter hours and found positive indications of a cairn, a pile of stones placed as a landmark, which indicated that humans indeed had previously scaled Katzimo. Ethnologist Hodge took along

Pasadena photographer Adam Clark Vroman to document his ascent.[9]

Earlier in July, Jo had mentioned in one of her letters a possible excursion to Acoma and Laguna and their hopes of arriving in time for Professor Libbey's ascent of Katzimo.

July 2

We still have one plan in view, or wish, I should say, that at present we do not see any hopes of being realized, and that is of stopping off at the station at Laguna in New Mexico in order to visit from there the wonderfully interesting Pueblo city of Acoma, some thirteen miles to the South, and near which, only three miles away and within plain sight of Acoma, is the "Enchanted Mesa" with the ruins of its ancient Pueblo city on its summit, for so many centuries beyond the reach of man and containing no one knows how many relics of untold value to the archaeological world.

Nan and Julie, you will remember Mr. Lummis' interesting story in connection with it in one of the recent *St. Nicholas* magazines entitled, "The Enchanted Mesa." Probably Nan didn't read it when I did, but I am sure Julie has. It is there where Professor William Libbey Jr. of Princeton is, according to the *N.Y. Sun*, to make his experiments with Mr. Eddy's tailess [sic] kites in order if possible to get a rope up and over the mesa, so that it may at last be possible to scale its smooth perpendicular height and discover what remains of the fated city on its summit.[10] You have probably seen more about the expedition in the New York papers than we can tell you from here, but if the expedition does not get started until the middle of August, instead of the middle of July, as the *N.Y. Sun* said was their intention, and if we could manage to visit Acoma and the Rock of Katzimo as the "Enchanted Mesa" is called, it would be mightily interesting to be there at the time of the expedition, even if we were only allowed to view their maneuvers at a distance.

But although Mr. Corser has assured us that he will give us a letter of introduction to the Presbyterian missionary who, with his wife (no doubt about the latter this time!) live at Laguna and who, he assured us more than once last Friday, would be only too glad to procure accommodations for us there. Still we do not want either Mr. Corser or our other friends here to think that we expect to travel about the country altogether dependent upon those Presbyterian missionaries, especially after having inquired, we discovered that there are no public accommodations whatever at Laguna. And consequently the aforesaid missionary's "finding us accommodations" would necessarily be in his own house which Mrs. Missionary might not find altogether as convenient as Mr. Corser may imagine. Still we have not given up all hope yet of visiting Acoma and "The Enchanted Mesa," so if you read in the papers our names in connection with those of Prof. Libbey and his party, as having made wonderful discoveries on the Rock of Katzimo . . .[11]

In Laguna the sisters met the Turkish-Jewish Presbyterian missionary, the Rev. Moses Bercovitz, who had arrived in New Mexico Territory in 1893 by way of Chile.[12] He and his family were a unique religious and cultural blend among the Pueblo Indian population and provided the girls with various kinds of support while there. With his help they were also able to visit Zuni, to the west of Laguna Pueblo. Unlike the sky cities of Walpi or Acoma, Zuni is low-lying and "sits beside a shallow river, which crawls silently over the sand like a flattened serpent." Near the river, the Zunis placed a pile of rocks near trader Douglas D. Graham's house in 1897, to mark the "center of the world."[13]

Minna romanticized about their adventures in three letters to her mother written from Laguna, Gallup, and Flagstaff.

Laguna, New Mexico
Friday, July 30, 1897

A letter of July 22 came from you, with an enclosed clipping about Prof. Libbey. I am so glad that you are having such a good time, and hope that the driving and fresh air will give you a good rest, for you must be tired by this time. Don't give too many dinners and things, will you? Just drive around and stay outdoors and rest and enjoy yourself.

You can't possibly be having such a good time as I am. I am happier than I ever deserved or ever shall deserve to be, for I have been to Acoma! To be sure, I have hardly seen enough of it to say that I have seen it; still I have been there. Up to yesterday, I counted the day that we went to the Colorado river as the best of this trip, but yesterday went ahead of it and of almost any single day that I can remember.

And now all my ambitions about the whole Southwest have condensed themselves into two things;—to spend any amount of time going to out-of-the-way places, and to stay awhile in Acoma. For there is hardly a corner of these thousands of square miles that is not worth enduring some hardship to see, but the most wonderful of all are the Grand Cañon and Acoma. I speak not from experience, but from firm conviction. At least all my memories and all my hopes are gathering about these two centers, for don't think that I am satisfied. This kind of travelling leaves one in the state of mind of the unsuccessful lover in some novels, who goes through life with an aching longing in his heart and thanks Providence each day for the cause of the ache. I have had enough good fortune to last a lifetime, but I am going to try my best so that it needn't last.

We started out yesterday morning: Jo, little Nathaniel Bercovitz, an Indian by the name of John Davis, and I. It is a twenty or twenty-five mile drive to Acoma, and the road goes within a quarter of a mile of the Mesa Encantada, which Prof. Libbey had explored six days before. Katzimo (Kaht-see´-mo), meaning Tall Rocky Place, the Indians call it, and that is a better name than any. We had heard the story of the explorations from Prof. Libbey in Flagstaff, and we heard it again from John, who did some or most of the pulling of the rope over the rock. Not himself, but with a team of horses. It seems that Prof. Libbey never really intended to use kites. He did make inquiries from Mr. Eddy, but finding them unsuitable gave up that plan and the rest is a newspaper story. They used a mortar or some such thing borrowed from the life saving service and shot their line completely over the southeast point of the mesa. John showed us where it fell.

The drive to Acoma is through unmistakable southwestern scenery; no one would ever take it for Pennsylvania, for instance. The broad mesa on which it is built lies in a great flat box of a valley floor almost as level as a quiet lake, sides nearly as steep as if cut straight downward with a knife. Here and there stand great perpendicular rocks, fantastically carved into countless caves and pillars; and huge rock tables, Katzimo among them, their straight sides rising from heaps of tumbled debris. We ate our lunch on a smooth shelf of one of the outlying pillars of the Acoma mesa. The side of the cliff has been worn away till its deep bays and jutting promontories have become one mass of dark cracks and smooth-worn hollows and pinnacles. Many of its old-time promontories have been entirely cut away—till now they stand alone. Between them and the main cliffs the wind has piled great hills of sand, and on some of these hills the people have built fences from rock to rock to make corrals for their cattle! I almost wish that I was an Acoma cow.

Up past the sand hills, the trail which we took dives into a shady crack behind a rock, and for the rest of the way it is a series of steps either cut in the solid rock or built with flat stones and tree trunks. It looks like the labor of years.

Half the children in Acoma came to meet us at the top of the rock, and the other half crowded around us the minute we had fairly reached the end of one of the long streets; some alone, some with a fat baby brother or sister slung in a shawl behind their backs, and one carefully hugging a small white puppy. We had brought a bag of stick candy with us (a borrowed idea), and the children who at first ran every time we looked at them soon forgot their shyness and stood around in an expectant circle, holding out their hands for the sugary sticks, or perhaps holding out the hands of the babies behind them. There doesn't seem to be any age limit to the candy craze in Acoma, for afterwards some elderly women held out their hands with much smiling and showing of teeth, and the little brown youngest was too small to know what those striped things were for. But he soon found out!

Several women and older girls came out on their first-story roofs to watch the first candy-giving. It made a picture not soon to be forgotten, the long blocks of three story, terraced houses, soft gray against a sky as blue as Italy ever dreamed of; the bright red dresses of the women gathered on the roofs, their faces half amused, half curious, and the silent crowd of plump brown children, watching our every movement from under their straight-cut black bangs, and talking to each other in hushed whispers as if this was a very solemn occasion. Almost all the people of Acoma are now in Acomita, their summer Pueblo, taking care of their crops; but two or three men, a few women, and a small crowd of children are left to take care of the herds and the town. You see they live in luxury, these people, with town and country houses and all sorts of style! I have not heard of any other Pueblo that has a summer annex, but there may be any number. (Zuñi has 2 or 3, and I think that many others have them.)

We walked around and admired the church and the graveyard and the houses and the ovens and in fact everything from the chimney-pots to the little gypsum windows, and everywhere we went the children trotted after us in a body. They grew very friendly, laughing and playing around and nearly getting themselves shut into the cameras in their eagerness to see whatever was going on. I think they were about the most good-natured and contented-looking group of children that I ever saw. And the older people were about the same.

We went and talked for a while to one woman who assured us that she could understand English, though I think that about all she could understand was "candy" and all her English speech was a nod of the head and a very broad smile. She and her daughter, a very pretty girl, sat on their roof and we stood in the street below with two or three other women and the children, of course. It was a very sociable group! Jo would ask John for the Indian version of whatever she wanted to say, and her remarks were received with a great deal of laughter (Juliette would say "enthusiastic cheering"), especially for efforts at getting the right pronunciation, for to an uninitiated outsider many of the Queres [Keres] consonants sound like nothing so much as sneezing, though the language is by no means harsh. Quite the contrary.[14] As for me, I was seized with a sudden attack of bashfulness and could do nothing but stand and smile, out loud sometimes. But the people are so good on the smile themselves that I doubt if they recognized my humble attempts.

Mrs. Bercovitz thinks that the Pueblos are not over clean, but they didn't impress me that way. Seems to me their instincts are all right, but in some ways Nature is against them. What can you expect in this land of sandstorms and barely enough water to live on; a place where every hard rain washes a cubic foot or so of mud plaster onto one's parlor floor, and where every drop of water for the family's use must be carried over half a mile of steep sand and rocks on the mother's head?[15] I do not think it is fair to compare them to ourselves, with our Boards of Health and sanitary laws and scientific investigations; but rather to other "civilized" races that are yet untouched by modern methods, or even to our own ancestors at a period which we consider far ahead of any Indian ideas. I don't think the Pueblos will suffer from any parallel comparison, even though they have no Dr. Emery [a professor?]. Some of them are so exquisitely neat in appearance as to make me actually ashamed of myself; and as for the children, it would take a phenomenal lot of washing to keep those lively youngsters looking like some of our babies, and there simply isn't time for it. And think of it, these people have worked out their own civilization alone and unaided, then look at some of the more backward European peoples that have had continual contact with the most advanced nations of the world to pull them forward—and you will admit that the Pueblos have done a pretty thorough piece of work.

Gallup, New Mexico August 5, Thursday

This is an unexpected heading, for it was only yesterday that we decided to come here. Mr. Bercovitz suggested it yesterday afternoon by saying that it was a pity that we were not going to Zuñi, and now, behold, we are going there. My, but I am glad! You see, Zuñi is one of the very few several-story pyramidal Pueblos now in existence—Taos is the only other one I know of—but though very anxious to see it we had thought it one of the impossibilities as it is not very near the railroad. But we have struck luck again. Mr. Bercovitz gave us a letter of introduction to the Congregational minister here (this seems to be a sort of Ministerial Relief expedition where the ministers do the relieving), and though he is out of town his wife received us with great hospitality, sent us to this comfortable boarding place, recommended a reliable liveryman, and told us we were just in time! Now there is nothing more pleasantly exciting to the eager sightseer than those words; and we nearly squealed with joy, for we had come to Gallup at a mere guess, thinking that if we couldn't take this interesting side trip, one day would not be lost in making sure that we couldn't, so that we should not be haunted by any "it-might-have-beens." I forgot to say that the reason we have so much extra time is that the Snake Dance does not take place until the 20th [21st], and our party starts on the 14th.

Well, our good fortune consists in the fact that Miss Denis [sic], one of the teachers in the Government school at Zuñi, is spending the day with Mrs. Simpkon, the minister's wife, and she is going to take us back with her to-morrow (Friday). We are going to stay over Sunday in the teachers' house, and come back Monday. How's that for fun? Moreover, there is a very important dance—something to do with rain—going on in Zuñi to-morrow, and we expect to be in time to see part of it, although we drive forty miles. Hurrah![16]

But I don't believe that it will be quite so much fun as Acoma;—quaint, substantial, yet only half-real Acoma, where all that I need to make me happy is to sit on the rocks and look and dream—because there is almost nothing that could be. We have been there again since the first of this letter was written, and it was better than the first time in everything except that it wasn't quite a first impression. We started out quite early Monday morning and came back Tuesday afternoon. Those were two days worth having! I can feel the sunshine of them now, can see the strange rock pinnacles against the misty coloring of the silent valley; can hear the children's voices round me and see the long irregular blocks of the queer old city.

Oh Acoma, I think you are enchanted and I too am under the spell. I wish I could live there awhile and study Indians and have enough rocks!

We stayed over night with one of the "first families," as Jo says, and I don't know who has treated us with the greatest kindness, our new white friends or the citizens of Acoma. We were the only white people for about twenty miles around and the only English-speaking people on the mesa, for John slept at the foot of the cliffs to be near the horses. It was great fun! And we saw so much more than we could possibly have seen in any other way.[17]

Our dinner Monday night was not served in courses; merely through oversight, I suppose, for it was a very good dinner, beginning with bread, after that more bread, then ending up with bread. You needn't think that the Hollenbacks are particularly advanced because they use whole wheat bread. Why, we had a whole dinner of it, that night in Acoma! All the Indian wheat flour is made of whole wheat, has been for centuries, and very nice flour it is, in spite of its being ground every grain by hand. It makes bread with a taste like your shredded wheat, and Mr. Graham (he's the Indian trader at Zuñi) says that the Zuñi wheat is better than any he ever saw in the American markets.

We thought that we had left our punkah-wallah in Kansas City;—but we found one again in the person of our hostess at Acoma. Do you know, she insisted on standing and waving off the flies all the time we were eating, and nothing could persuade her to stop, or to eat anything herself, —till we thought of the jam. That jam of Mrs. Bercovitz's carried the day. We began on the children, then I gave Mrs. Docita my chair and Jo offered her some bread and jam, and pretty soon we were all sitting around feasting on bread and jam; that is, all except the father and the son and heir, who were off working in the fields and were only home at night. The son and heir was a boy of about thirteen, with fluffy-scruffems hair, exceedingly clean clothes and a great deal of dignity. I don't know whether he disapproved of us or whether this was the first year he had been allowed to work in the fields and he was therefore feeling his own importance; but that child and the old man who stopped our first day's picture-taking were the only Pueblos we have seen who wouldn't smile. It was a most cordial family that that child belonged to, but he sat in a chair and regarded us with a solemn stare every minute that he was in the house; except at night, and then truth compels me to admit that he snored. We tried to get him to relax his dignity a little; but every time I smiled at him I felt as if a reproving voice had said: "Why is this unseemly levity?" so I gave it up.

Flagstaff, August 12, Thursday

The only style of letter that I can manage to get off seems to be the patchwork variety, so that it is a mercy that I do not send very many or else you would be kept busy saying "chestnuts" to my news. I have been having some fun this morning, I can tell you! Fifteen days' mail makes a feast almost equal to the pounded dried meat cooked with corn that they gave us at Acoma.[18] Nan says that she and Papa are uncertain about our address. They needn't be, for it is always the same: New Bank, Flagstaff. When we are away from here it is either in regions where there is no p.o., or else the time of our being at any particular place is so uncertain that we don't even have our mail forwarded. I suppose the reason that we didn't let any one know of this was because we thought that everything would be sent to the given address until we sent word of another one.

I had six letters waiting for me this morning; two fatties from you, written at Canton [Ohio], July 28 and Paul Smith's, Aug. 2; two from Louise (and Julie); one from Nan, July 26, and one from the Chicken, which I enclose. Seems to me it would have been more polite to write to you if he wanted to know when he might come to your house. I never did understand the way some men have of writing to the daughter when the mother has asked them to visit, but perhaps it is the correct thing, is it? I will send an answer to the Chicken by the next mail and I hope he'll forgive the more than three weeks delay, as it was unavoidable.[19]

I don't wonder that Nan thought we were not going to Acoma, from the alternating hopeful and despondent reports we sent home; but perhaps she forgot that Acoma is a living Pueblo and not a fictitious heap of ruins on top of the Enchanted Mesa. All the Pueblo tribes used to have a habit of building new towns and abandoning their old ones whenever they had reason to do so,—though the movings might be hundreds of years apart,—and as there was generally no reason for tearing down the houses many of the old walls are standing still, especially those that are protected by cliffs or caves.

The country about Zuñi is dotted with small ruined Pueblos, all once homes of that tribe. Now the legend of the Enchanted Mesa said that on its top old Acoma was builded, that is, the town preceding the present one. If the story had been true, Prof. Libbey would have found an old Pueblo like the rest, only it would have had the advantage of being ruined only by the weather and not at all by the hand of man, and of containing many household utensils that had not been carried away, as usual, by moving families. It would have been a flourishing live Pueblo suddenly cut off from its people and all the rest of the world, battered by time, but still not [a] dismantled, war-scarred, relic-hunted pile of stones that we see oftenest, for poor old Father Time gets the credit for a good many misdeeds whose blame we might put nearer home. I wish it had been true!

Old Katzimo stands as serene and unchanging in his rocky majesty as he did in the days when the passing stranger gazed with awe at his untrodden summit and grew silent in the shadow of those silent walls. The sunshine that falls about him is enchanted still, for he and his brother mesas, great world-pillars, are chief monuments of the beauty of all that wonder-region,—and who shall say that is not enough?

Don't pity me for the end of this summer, for to tell the truth, it had never entered my head to pity myself. It is all too much mine, if you know what I mean. There are some kinds of happiness that we do not consciously come to nor leave; they are always with us. I do not any longer feel a sadness in leaving Brooklyn or Glen Summit or Wilkes-Barre; I belong to all of them, and live among them all. So it is here, only in less degree. I declare that I never thought of this as a separate trip, a thing to be accomplished once for all, like some people's longed-for trips to Europe,—or if I ever thought so, that is long past.

It seems as natural as Lakewood, indeed sometimes I can hardly believe that I have never been here before.[20] Everything I ever read or imagined about these places,—and there was little enough of the former—went together into one long dream, and part of the time I lived in that dream as a person may in his castles in Spain. And when that dream turned into solid reality before my eyes,—well, at first I felt a little bit wild, like a stable horse suddenly turned out to pasture.

I suppose I kept stiller than usual, but there were times when I wanted to dance jigs and shout as hard as I could. To see those flat-topped mesas and little cañons with their bare, sun-heated cliffs and know that they were not mere pictures in my brain, to see the long ladders leaning against the terraced communal houses with their gray plastered walls and queer pottery chimneys, and find that I could walk up them—I wouldn't give the memory of that sensation for all the wonders of the Arabian Nights. But the things themselves didn't seem queer, only the fact that they were real. The first hour in a new place I generally spend looking at something and saying to myself, "There it is, it's real!" as if I had been around the world searching for that particular object. After a day or two I am simply in a state of absolute contentment, so I am now and so I shall be at home. I don't think a four days journey east will quite take me away from this place, any more than now I can feel myself entirely separate from home.

If I was alone and friendless do you know what I should like to do? Come out here for a few years and study southwestern ethnology and archaeology and geology and a few things of that sort.

My what fun! I want to find out a little something at home when I have a chance. The Lord willing, I am coming out here again sometime, and if not, at least I can have a good time studying. So be glad with me dear, but don't waste your pity even for the end that is not an end, for with me the thought of it does not cause a regret when I think of getting ready to learn something. It strikes me that this is getting to be pretty full of Minna.

Somehow when you started for the Adirondacks I didn't realize that you were starting a rival attraction to the Great American Trip. I enjoyed your attentive landlords and "village maids" in quite an unprejudiced way until it came to your holding onto trees while the horses progressed through the mud at the rate of two miles an hour; then I concluded that the competition was getting too close. We haven't been treated to any experiences like that! I am afraid Mr. Wilcox [the liveryman] didn't treat us fairly; he should have thrown in a few excitements. Don't you want to sell out and let me tell your stories? My stock is getting low; though come to think of it, it would hardly do for me to talk of the palatial mansions, stately elms or velvet lawns of this part of Arizona. Trees and lawns are an imposition anyhow. What does anyone want more than a flat-roofed adobe house, a stretch of sand, some sagebrush, a few cacti and perhaps an occasional cedar?

We were glad to hear of the success of Nan's fair. Do you suppose Mr. George [founder of the Junior Republic] got his idea of a little republic within the big one from an Indian Pueblo?

"I suppose that you are now in the midst of your family circle in Glen Summit," as Jo's friends are fond of writing to her. My, but the circle must be glad. Wait until September, and we will make it a little larger. . . .

I should like to wish Mabel and Julie good luck with their century puzzle. And please, Mama dear, take your own advice and don't write such long letters. . . (P.S. We are b.w. & h. [both well and happy]).[21]

Minna Hollenback returned many times to New Mexico. In 1932, at age fifty-five, she built the adobe house she had envisioned thirty-five years earlier. The massive Santa Fe house would have no green velvet lawn to soak up precious water, which the Southwest Indians regarded as sacred, and at its completion the San Ildefonso Indians from the Rio Grande area came and danced the Eagle Dance. Together they celebrated the blessing of the house and a lasting friendship. Minna remembered her Southwest Indian friends to her dying words at age ninety-two: "They're all back at the reservation."[22]

Notes

1. Anthropologist Frank Hamilton Cushing, who stayed at Zuni from 1879 to 1884, spelled the sacred dance Keá-k´ok-shi. Cushing, *Zuni*.

2. Bloom, ed., "Bourke on the Southwest," 373; Lummis, "Three Weeks in Wonderland," 111–12.

3. See Simmons, *Following the Santa Fe Trail*. Passengers for Santa Fe arrive at Lamy, 14 miles south of the city. The train station was named for Jean-Baptiste Lamy, the nineteenth-century French archbishop in the Southwest.

4. In 1898 Minna and Jo's parents traveled to Alamogordo, N.M., from New York on a private railroad car belonging to entrepreneur Charles Bishop Eddy. They had been his guests in 1897 at an elaborate dinner party given at the Waldorf to attract Eastern investors in his El Paso & Northeastern Railroad and in the coalfields of Dawson, N.M., near Raton.

5. Letters and diaries of nineteenth-century travelers frequently mention the prairie dog-owl cohabitation.

6. There were four Pecos mission churches. The ruins visible today from Interstate 25, twenty-five miles southeast of Santa Fe, are those of the fourth church, the second having been destroyed during the Pueblo Revolt of 1680. The site is now a national monument. See Hayes, *The Four Churches of Pecos*.

7. JH to father, June 10, 1897, HC. In Kansas City, Minna and Jo purchased *The Spanish Pioneers* by Charles F. Lummis. (This book enjoyed sixteen editions.) For his contributions to Spanish colonial history, Lummis was knighted with the rank of commander in the royal order of Isabela la Católica from Spain's King Alphonso XIII. Fiske and Lummis, *Charles F. Lummis*, 121.

8. Lummis, *Mesa, Cañon and Pueblo*, 214, 222. For accounts of the Libbey Katzimo ascent, see the *New York Times*, July 25, 27, 1897; the *Albuquerque Morning Democrat*, Aug. 19, 1897; Lummis, "The Disenchanted Libbey," 200–201. Princeton University's Museum of Natural History wrote the author that "Professor Libbey's southwestern trip was entirely unknown to us." Baird to author, Sept. 18, 1984. Information, photographs (noted in one newspaper account), and any other material relating to Libbey's Katzimo experience appear to be missing from his papers in Clark University Archives, Worcester, Mass.

9. Hodge, "Katzimo the Enchanted," 225–36; Mahood, ed., *Photographer of the Southwest: Adam Clark Vroman*, 31–34; Webb and Weinstein, *Dwellers at the Source*, 150. Vroman also photographed Minna and Jo Hollenback at Acoma in front of the house of former Acoma Governor Solomon Bibo and his wife, Juana Valle. (See n. 17 below.)

10. According to the *New York Times*, July 18, 1897, and the *Princeton News*, June 19, 1897,

Professor Libbey did indeed contemplate using William J. Eddy's aerial kites. See also Wise, "Experiments with Kites," 78–86.

11. JH to parents, July 2 to 4, 1897, HC.

12. Educated in Switzerland, Bercovitz served six years as a missionary in the Southwest. He did not speak English or the Laguna language fluently, but he was ahead of his time in believing that the natives should worship in their own language. During his tenure in New Mexico Territory, he translated a hymnbook into Laguna with the help of a young Laguna boy who had attended the Carlisle Indian School in Carlisle, Pa. According to Capt. C. E. Nordstrom (the acting Indian agent) and unknown to Bercovitz, the translator included several obscene couplets in a hymn, which were discovered by an outraged tribal patriarch before publication. Bercovitz wrote to Washington, D.C., in an effort to get his 8-page "Lexicon of Conversation" in the Laguna language (a three-year project) published, but it is not known if he was successful. Bercovitz to Powell, Feb. 25, 1896, SAA.

13. Trader Douglas D. Graham, born in New York in 1849, was appointed a temporary teacher at Zuni in August 1882. U.S. Dept. of the Interior, *Annual Report of the Commissioner of Indian Affairs for 1882*, 129. In 1881 he opened a store in Zuni, selling out in 1898 to Samuel T. Toner of Gallup. He repurchased it only a year later, then again sold it to a former partner, James W. Bennett. Graham became the first superintendent of the U.S. Indian Agency for Zuni in 1902. McNitt, *Indian Traders*, 240; Bloom, ed., "Bourke on the Southwest," 477. Graham often entertained his guests with a ladder-climbing performance by his dog; all dogs of the multistoried pueblos, and Indian children as well, ran up and down ladders with amazing agility and speed, which was the only way to reach the upper stories. Bloom, ed., "Bourke on the Southwest," 192. For a contemporaneous account of Zuni, see author Hamlin Garland's description of it in 1895, "A Day at Zuni," in Underhill and Littlefield, Jr., *Hamlin Garland's Observations on the American Indian*, 112–13.

14. Acoma is the largest pueblo of the Keresan linguistic group. It also claims to be the oldest continuously inhabited city in the United States. See Minge, *Acoma: Pueblo in the Sky*.

15. Rainwater was the only water available on Acoma mesa itself.

16. There were two women by the name of Dennis, perhaps sisters, listed at Zuni in 1897–1898: "Miss Fannie J. Dennis, matron, and Miss Ella P. Dennis, assistant matron." "Report of Field Matron in Zuni Pueblo," U.S. Dept. of the Interior, *Annual Report of the Commissioner of Indian Affairs . . . 1898*, 208.

17. In Acoma the sisters probably spent the night with the Solomon Bibo family. Bibo, a trader since 1882 at Acoma and one of three brothers who were sons of a Jewish rabbi, married an Acoma woman named Juana Valle and served as governor of Acoma in 1886. Parish, Errata of "The German Jew," 150; Minge, *Acoma*, 65.

18. The "pounded dried meat" Minna and Jo ate at Acoma is called jerky; it is still part of the New Mexican diet today.

19. The identity of "Chicken" is unknown.

20. Lakewood, N.J., was the home of the Hollenback sisters' maternal grandparents, the Eli Beards.

21. ABH to mother, July 30, Aug. 5, Aug. 12, 1897, HC.

22. Interview with Dorothy Twyeffort Hubbell, 1982.

Chapter Seven
Snakes, Huggers, and Photographers at Hopi

———◆———

Near six o'clock the evening of August 21, 1897, twelve Antelope priests solemnly moved past the Snake kiva of the Hopi village of Walpi. Ancient religious tradition dictated that each priest toss a pinch of sacred cornmeal into the underground opening of the kiva as the Indian ceremony, centuries old and timed by the summer sun, was about to begin.

Bedecked Indians and non-Indians alike ringed the small, packed-earth dance plaza clinging to the east side of the village. Surrounded by countless photographers attempting to record in the fading sunlight this ancient rite for rain, the Snake Dance began to a throbbing drumbeat. During the public ceremony that lasted less than an hour, dancing Snake priests, assisted by "huggers" holding eagle feathers, controlled the renegade snakes, but no such restraint had yet been devised for the visitor with a camera. Ultimately, the photographers and non-Indians would prove to be an intolerable intrusion into the Indians' sacred-dance world.

The Snake Dance is a Hopi ceremonial prayer for rain to nourish their crops. Snakes are caught, danced with, entrusted with the rain petitions of the people, and then released on the desert to carry their messages to the deities. Of both mythical and historical origin, the Snake Legend has been passed down through generations of Hopis for a long, long time, a time without beginning, or "very, very when."[1]

The Snake Legend

Very, very when, Tiyo (meaning boy in Hopi), the eldest son of a village chief, haunted the edge of some cliffs and often pondered the destination of the water flowing through the bottom of the gorge. His father would say, "It must flow down some great pit, into the underworld, for after all these years the gorge below never fills up, and none of the water ever flows back again. Maybe it goes so far away that many old men's lives would be too short to mark its return." Finally, Tiyo's curiosity became too great, and he decided, against his family's wishes, that he must follow the flowing water.

Reluctantly, Tiyo's father hollowed out the trunk of a cottonwood tree in which Tiyo could float down the river, giving him pahos or prayer emblems for the gods of the underworld and down from an eagle's thigh. The father told his son that the Spider Woman would show him how to use these things. After countless days of floating, Tiyo went ashore where he found a small round hole in the ground called the sipapu, the place of emergence of all people. From the hole he heard, "sist, sist," repeated four times. He then heard the Hopi greeting, "Umpituh," or "You have arrived." Tiyo then descended through the hole into the house of the Spider Woman.

On the fifth morning, Spider Woman gave nahu, a charm liquid, to Tiyo, which he was to put on the tip of his tongue and spew upon angry guards of the kivas or rooms he must visit. Spider Woman invisibly perched herself on top of Tiyo's right ear to be his prompter throughout his journey into the underworld. She told him to take some eagle down in his hand and step upon the sipapu to descend into the underworld. This he did.

Once in the underworld, Tiyo met the great snake named Gatoya who, after being spewed with nahu, allowed them to pass. Pahos were given to the different gods visited, Tawa, the Sun, telling Tiyo that the blessing he would most prize would be the rain-cloud he would receive from the chief of the Snake-Antelope kiva. In the evening light of the fifth day, Tiyo went into the snake kiva where he sat for four days, listening to the teachings of the chief. Tiyo was told, "Here we have sun dance of rain and corn; in your land is but little; so thus shall you use the nahu; fasten these prayers in your breast; and these are the songs you shall sing and these the pahos you shall make; and when you display the white and the black on your bodies the clouds will come."

The chief gave Tiyo two young maidens, one of whom he must give to his younger brother, who knew the charm which prevents death from the bite of the rattlesnake. Tiyo took the maidens to his mother's house where their hair was washed and their feast announced from a house-top; even today the snake feast is announced in this manner.

On the fifth day of the ceremony and for three succeeding days, low clouds came and snake people from the underworld came and went into the kivas. Later, the snake people metamorphosed into reptiles on the desert. And on the ninth morning, the snake maidens asked the younger brothers (the Snake society) to go out and bring all the snakes, wash their heads and dance with them. When this was done, the snakes were covered with sacred prayer-meal and carried to the desert where they returned to the Snake kiva of the underworld with the petitions for rain.[2]

"To Moqui-land" was how Minna Hollenback entitled the photographs in her album of the trip to the Hopi Snake Dance in 1897. Unfortunately, she left no letters or diary entries telling of her adventures in Hopi; we have only her photographs and captions.

Many people called the Hopi Indians Moquis or Moki, the latter a name they neither called themselves nor liked because it meant "the dead ones." The name may have come from the sixteenth-century Spaniards or possibly the Paiute Indian word *Moqwi*. The Hopis call themselves *Hopituh Shinumu*, meaning "the peaceful ones." They are gentle people blessed with humor, and along with this humor they also possess a deep spiritual quality evident even to a stranger.[3]

Strangers invaded Hopiland in late August more than any other time of year to witness the Snake Dance. Droves of strangers first began to come from all across the United States in 1897, carrying cameras to capture what some irreverently called the "sacred hop." That year proved to be a watershed year at Walpi for the convergence of some of America's best-known Southwest photographers: Adam Clark Vroman, George Wharton James, Frederick Hamer Maude, Frederick Monsen, and George Ben Wittick. Photography during the Snake Dance became an irritation the Hopi tolerated until 1913, when they initiated a ban that became effective by the late 1920s. As a consequence, cameras are no longer allowed at any Pueblo Indian ceremonials, and today, non-Indians are not permitted to watch the Snake Dance.[4]

The Snake Dance at Walpi on First Mesa was considered to be the largest and most dramatic of any of those danced on the three Hopi mesas. The villages alternated years, with Walpi in the odd-numbered; it was considered the photographer's plum during the 1890s. Among the photographers there in 1897, heretofore all men, was Amelia Beard Hollenback, a young amateur from Brooklyn. Her photographs of the Walpi ceremony may well be some of the earliest ever taken of it by a woman, but they were not discovered until ten years after her death in August 1969. Coincidentally, that same month and year also marked the last Snake Dance performed in the village of Walpi. A close examination of numerous cross-plaza photographs indicates no other woman photographing the 1897 dance.[5]

On August 15, 1897, before leaving Flagstaff for Hopi on their ten-day desert camping trip, Minna and Jo prudently paid a visit to a local physician, a Dr. Robinson. The previous day they had purchased a bottle and a half of an unnamed medicine, two bottles of mariani, a bottle of cascara sagrada (a nineteenth-century cure-all), and pepsin. The medicines were remedies for the contingencies of being Victorian women camping on the desert with little or no water or privacy, as well as the possible effects of strange food in a remote area.[6]

Prudently, the sisters also cashed checks for $25.00 in silver for any necessary remuneration to the Indians, who preferred silver coins to paper money, using them to decorate their clothing and to make jewelry (the going rate in the 1890s was $2.00 for every $1.00 of coin silver). For "tenderfoot easterners," Minna and Jo quickly caught on to the ways of the West, especially when it came to money, although they obviously felt vulnerable as single women. Minna writes a humorous and candid description of the fierce competition for the tourists' silver dollars by non-Indians, who lined the inside of their pockets with them.[7]

July 22, 1897
Finished July 28

These Westerners, some of them, have an insatiate desire to make their fortune off the tenderfoot East, but all you have to do is to stand on your dignity, be rather indifferent and undecided, and they come down from their pedestals as quickly as an Italian seller of tortoise shell. Before we went to the Verde a man came around and kindly offered to take us two there for $12 a day, while the five of us finally went in only a little less luxury for a little over $7 a day! Old Mr. Wilcox, who took us, told us that he "didn't think much of a man who would take advantage that way," (remark called forth by a funny incident on the road), and I really do think that he treated us fairly and did his best, in spite of his "heart failure" and his rickety old turnout [carriage].[8]

We have been having a like funny experience about the Snake Dance. Oh the wire-pulling and lobbying that goes on for the sake of one extra stroke of business! One man has actually been trying to buy up the whole town so that no one can go to the Snake Dance except in his party; and what's more, he has nearly succeeded. He is managing a big party for Mr. Riordan (the Riordans are the great people of this neighborhood) and he has been working for nearly a week to make us join it. I'm going to ask Mr. D. M. [Riordan] for some reliable information, for the zealous Mr. Hoxworth has told us so many up-and-down whoppers that we can't depend on him. "Why, I was showing D. M. the figures, and they came to $400 more than he expected"; but he said "That's all right, Harry! Take the wagon right down to the train and meet the senators." The town is hardly large enough to hold Mr. H. now that he is managing an important party with several celebrities in it. You would think that he was Master of the Horse for the King of Siam. I suppose he wants us to be company for the other celebrities.[9]

That reminds me, I forgot to explain that there are three Messrs. Riordan and instead of always going by their last name they are usually known as Mr. D. M. [Denis Matthew], Mr. Mike [Michael James], and Mr. Tim [Timothy Allen]. Even the Mrs. Riordans are known by these same names! The Riordan party are going to take a long trip, from 20 to 30 days, beginning with the Snake Dance and ending with Cataract Cañon [in Grand Canyon], and I wonder if you would forgive us if we took the whole thing? We are thinking of it, or else of coming straight back from the S.D. [Snake Dance] and going to the Natural Bridge [in Verde Valley]. The S.D. alone takes from ten days to two weeks, and as we may not start for that until the 10th, we shall probably not be home as soon as we had expected. In fact, we have already applied for an extension of our tickets, in case we should run a few days over the original limit of Sept. 2. We do so want to see what we can. Now you have no idea of the endless powwowing that must be gone through with before every trip. If we were a family it would be very different; but we have to depend more or less on other people, and our easy and comfortable road is actually paved with plans that "fell through."

Prof. Libbey wrote to Jo, saying that he had heard from Mr. A. [from Brooklyn] asking if he could be of use to us and inquiring what arrangements were being made in Flagstaff to visit the S.D. After this kindness on his part and Mr. A's, the least we could do was to tell him what he asked. My dear, we have spent nearly half our time for six days in planning and inquiring; Mrs. Olney has done much more than we, and the visible fruits of it are that we can go with the Riordan party at $4.00 a day apiece, and perhaps Prof. Libbey and his friend Mr. Bridgeman [from Brooklyn] also if they let them know in time. Bah! We did have rosy prospects of a party of eight or nine that would go independently, as quickly, comfortably and inexpensively as possible—Oh joy! Oh rapture! They are going! I beg their pardons, those friends whom I was going to accuse of backing out one by one. It did seem as if we were being left alone in our glory; but while I was maligning them they were going ahead and actually engaging our teams; at least two of them were, Mr. Clark and Mr. [John W.] Francis. Mrs. Olney came in to tell us that Mr. Thurber (proprietor of the Grand Cañon hotel and stage line) would take us for $3.00 a day apiece, everything included except bedding, and make the trip in ten or eleven days. If

Prof. Libbey and Mr. Bridgeman will join us we shall be only too glad; but the Albuquerque paper has a very disheartening three-column article headed "Disenchanted Mesa," beginning with the cheerful news that the mesa was successfully scaled and not a sign of human habitation found, and ending by the statement that Prof. L. and Mr. B. will spend a few days at the Cañon and then go directly East. So perhaps they have given up their plan of attending the S.D., and perhaps they haven't.[10]

Of two possible routes to Hopi from Flagstaff in 1897, one was to "pull sand," as it was called in Arizona, going by wagon the entire 134 miles, and the other was to take the train to Canyon Diablo and then pull sand for the remaining desert miles. Apparently, the Hollenback party chose the latter route of approximately 103 miles from the railroad tracks to Walpi. The horse trail was always shorter, and the smaller the party, of course, the faster and lighter the travel, with fewer stomachs to fill. New Mexico photographer Ben Wittick, who also attended the 1897 Walpi Snake Dance, wrote that he had a difficult time getting to Hopi because water was scarce and the roads "awful sandy."[11]

Tourist business was already becoming big business in Arizona Territory. By 1898 Frederick W. Volz, financially backed by well-known trader Don Lorenzo Hubbell of Ganado on the Navajo Reservation, owned three trading posts between the railroad stop at Canyon Diablo and the Hopi village of Oraibi on Third Mesa. These stores sometimes served, in the true spirit of nineteenth-century Arizonan hospitality, as overnight stops, with guests sleeping on countertops and among the inventory.[12]

One of the difficulties of camping and traveling was carrying enough food. Minna noted in her expense diary the purchase of canned goods, known as "airtights" in the West, at Volz's store en route. Canned food purchased earlier in Flagstaff by the Hollenback sisters included St. Charles milk (four cans for $.70); olives (four bottles for $1.05); chicken (three cans for $1.65); calves foot jelly ($.70 a bottle); and malted milk ($1.00 a bottle). Much against her principles, but having learned that traveling the Arizona desert created strange bedfellows, Minna was forced to purchase additional canned food after arriving at Hopi from the zealous Mr. Hoxworth.[13]

The wagon roads from Flagstaff to Hopi crossed the Little Colorado River many miles east of its western rendezvous with the Colorado River in Grand Canyon. Along these primitive highways of Arizona, a phenomenon existed of stacking the inevitable empty tins following each meal, a tin-can litany as it were. Minna entitled a photograph of empty cans from a recent repast, which were turned upside down on sticks, "Starvation Camp." A German scientist traveling the Painted Desert at the turn of the century once declared that all of

Arizona Territory would baffle future geologists with its border-to-border stratum of tin.[14]

The tin-strewn roads from Flagstaff to Hopi passed the red mesa, a dominant landmark on the Painted Desert, today known as Newberry Mesa (called Kachina Points by the Hopis), and followed the Oraibi Wash northward. At this red mesa the Navajo Reservation, which surrounds the Hopi Reservation and must be crossed in order to reach Walpi, is a flat landscape that in minutes can turn into a gummy sea of red mud carved by arroyos of rushing water. No matter how laborious, pulling sand in a wagon was much to be preferred over the quicksand-like mud.

By noon the third day, the Hollenback group reached Big Burro Spring (south of Oraibi), nestled on the east bank of the Oraibi Wash. This secluded spring, approximately sixty miles north of Canyon Diablo, consisted of watering troughs and a pitched tin-roof adobe house, the latter a gift of the federal government. The travelers stopped here overnight at a house owned by Honani, a Hopi Indian. The highway today between Leupp and Oraibi generally follows the Hollenback 1897 route. In September 1986 Honani's house still stood at Big Burro Spring, with ruins of other buildings nearby. The area today is shaded by aging cottonwoods and remains much the same as pictured in Minna's photos.[15]

Honani, known as the Friendly Chief of Shongopovi on Second Mesa, had traveled in 1890 to Washington, D.C., with Lololomai of Old Oraibi on Third Mesa and Simo and Ahnawita of Walpi and Sichomovi on First Mesa, to talk with the white man's leaders about Navajo encroachment on their land. Ignoring the heated land boundary issue with the Navajos, the U.S. officials attempted to persuade the Hopis to move off their isolated mesa-tops down to the low-lying areas surrounding the mesas, in the naive hope of better controlling the Hopi Indians. They also wished the Indians to send their children to the Keams Canyon school. The Hopis have been the most successful of the Pueblo Indians in resisting religious and cultural influence since the Spaniards arrived in the sixteenth century. A principal reason for this is the total isolation of the Hopi mesas.

The houses on the desert floor surrounding the three Hopi mesas were the Indians' reward for pledging cooperation with the government. They might well be considered the first government housing project in U.S. history. The red pitched-roof adobe houses, called *palakikis* in the Hopi language, were a nineteenth-century version of housing similar to what is seen today on Southwest reservations. Heretofore, Indian roofs had traditionally been flat and made of mud. Anyone who has ever lived beneath a flat mud roof knows the hazards only too well—numerous leaks with every rainstorm and possible collapse of the hundreds of pounds of dirt used as roofing, a certain death for the dweller.[16]

The Hollenback sisters and Mrs. Olney may have slept inside Honani's palakiki, while the men bedded down outside under the cottonwood trees surrounding Big Burro Spring, keeping a watchful eye for any stray snakes that might have eluded the Hopis in their hunt for the approaching dance (in Indian lore the snake guards their most precious commodity, water). Once on the hot, dry desert, it is easy to understand why early southwestern routes were measured in spring-to-spring miles as a matter of survival, the travelers often competing with snakes for water. Unlike the miles measured from the comfort of a railroad car, those by wagon were seemingly endless. Seasoned Arizona campers, nevertheless, made the distances far more tolerable with their entertaining stories.

"Ma" Olney, the cheery Flagstaff schoolteacher, went along on the camping trip as chaperon. Without her motherly presence, which helped put the group of strangers at ease, Minna and Jo might have been forced to join the all-male Riordan party of celebrities; that group included at least one congressman from the East. [17]

Of the seven Arizona men who accompanied Minna, Jo, and Ma, the "Kentucky Cunnel" (Minna apparently spelled it the way he pronounced it) appeared in many of twenty-year-old Minna's photographs. Frank C. Reid, also twenty, was then an eligible bachelor. He sang bass in the Flagstaff Presbyterian choir, read law, led the campaign to restore Montezuma Castle in 1897, and eventually became a Presbyterian missionary, helping to found Ganado Mission on the Navajo Reservation.[18]

Among the other men in the Hollenback party was the Rev. Harry Corser of Flagstaff, in his natty camping attire topped by a straw hat. And looking as gentlemanly as ever was J. Wilbur Thurber, of the Grand Canyon stage, and Elias S. Wilcox, survivor of the Hollenback all-ladies' escapade to the Verde Valley. "Old Mr. Wilcox," as Minna called him, was in fact Judge Wilcox, an elected police judge in Flagstaff. A friend once described him: "He was a livery stable man, with round stomach and big moustache, was snappy and full of pep. Nobody escaped this judge without contributing something for the good and welfare of the town treasury."[19] The three remaining members of the party were John William Francis of Flagstaff, J. W. Walker of Phoenix, and an unknown Indian. A more colorful but unlikely group of strangers never crossed the Painted Desert of Arizona together. These men who accompanied Minna and Jo to the Snake Dance deserve greater scrutiny. The western man, often attired in a dusty vest with a shirt and tie, seems to have held a certain intellectual attraction for eastern Minna.

The Reverend Corser remained only a year in Flagstaff as a Presbyterian missionary, not long enough to take up any wild western habits (attributed by some Flagstaffians to the bad blood that had moved west from Dodge City, Kansas). Flagstaff's earlier ministers, like some of its leading citizens, often took part in street fights, according to one account. One parishioner recalled that he separated two ministers of the gospel; one of them had gone as far as to take off his coat, fold it neatly and place it to one side on the ground. The fragile-looking but apparently hardy Corser moved to Alaska in 1898 to become a Protestant Episcopalian missionary for the next thirty years. There he published a short history of Alaska, plus a book on Eskimo giant totem poles.[20]

A man bent on an entirely different mission in the West was the one Minna called "Mr. Francis"—Sheriff John Francis. He is often pictured poised in a gunfighter's stance with a beady eye toward the camera. Francis became famous as a role model for Zane Grey in his novel *To the Last Man*, which is the story of the 1887 Tewksbury-Graham feud between rustlers and ranchers in Yavapai County, Arizona, where Francis served as undersheriff. By his death in 1925, he was a U.S. marshal. His obituary stated that "when he went after a man, he went to get him. His failures to accomplish his mission were few. Cool, brave, unhesitating, quick as a flash on the trigger, and a dead-shot, there were few among the numerous badmen of those days who cared to measure gun skill with him, and many of them, wiser than they were good, surrendered without a fight when he caught up with them. Some others, less discreet, tried to shoot it out, and in those cases Sheriff Francis was invariably victor." In early Flagstaff, John Francis taught what was sure to have been a well-disciplined classroom, drawing draft after hours at a local saloon.[21]

The group moved northeastward from Big Burro Spring across Hopi fields of corn (planted in sand dunes to capture water), around the southern tip of Second Mesa to the foot of First Mesa to a place called the Gap—Walpi. Of this fortress village, author D. H. Lawrence wrote, "Walpi stands in half-ruin high, high on a narrow rock-top where no leaf of life ever was tender. It is all grey, utterly dry, utterly pallid, stone and dust, and very narrow. Below it all the stark light of the dry Arizona sun." Lawrence attended a snake dance in the 1920s.[22]

In the early afternoon glare of August 20, Minna, Jo, and Mrs. Olney mounted their burros (probably a first for all three women) and, escorted by the men on foot, began ascending the 600-foot-high mesa to the village of Tewa, called Hano by the Hopis, at the top. It was founded by Tewa Indians from the Rio Grande area of northern New Mexico, after the Pueblo Revolt of 1680. In the village of Hano lived the expert Hopi potters, including Nampeyo, whose pottery Amelia Hollenback later collected.

Before reaching Walpi on slender First Mesa, the travelers passed through a second village called Sichomovi, meaning "the mound of flowers." From Sichomovi the group then crossed the narrow gap southward to the fingertip village of Walpi to make preparations for watching and photographing the Antelope Dance, which would take place at dusk that same day.

By midafternoon the Indians of Walpi were busily sweeping the dirt dance area and building the *kisi*, the temporary altar made of green-leafed cottonwood boughs. A conical structure made of poles covered with boughs, the kisi faced south toward the mushroom-shaped sacred rock at the southerly end of the dance area. In front of the opening, the Indians place a heavy plank with a hole representing the *sipapu* (place of emergence). Then began several hours of patient waiting and socializing for the spectators.

The Antelope Dance, which Minna called the Corn Dance in 1897, which she did not photograph, could be termed a dress rehearsal for the Snake Dance that occurred the following day at the same time and with the same dancers. During the Antelope Dance, the dancers hold ears of green corn in their mouths instead of snakes, no doubt the reason she called it the Corn Dance. There were far fewer spectators for this dance because no live, often poisonous snakes were used in the ceremonial. Both the Antelope and Snake Dances made up the two, then-public portions of the nine-day religious ceremony. In his discussion of the symbolism of the Snake Dance, Dr. Jesse Walter Fewkes, who was with the Smithsonian's Bureau of American Ethnology, related that the dance is a rain-making observance, tinged with sun worship. "To these must now be added corn or seed germination, growth and maturity, implied in the somewhat misleading name 'Corn-Dance,' a dominating influence in every great rite of Tusayan." He believed the snake to be a totemic personation (of clan relationship) to re-create ancestral "conditions" as found in the Hopi Snake Legend.[23]

Overlooking the fifteen- by twenty-seven-foot dance plaza, the second-story room with an adjacent rooftop rented by Minna and Jo turned out to be the best accommodations available at Walpi. The cost was $1.00 a night per person, breakfast included. As Minna commented, the one great risk, apart from the snakes themselves, was that of standing on a crowded mud roof. Roofs collapsed from time to time from too much weight, but only the stouthearted relished standing on the dance-plaza level where a snake might dart into the crowd during the dance, creating utter havoc.[24]

To photograph the Snake Dance on the 21st, Minna found a small, slightly elevated area at the north end of the cramped plaza, where she set up her camera and tripod. She stood close enough to a pole-ladder to the second-story rooftop to make a rapid retreat possible, if necessary. A desirable photographic vantage point in such a confined area proved no easy task for a novice elbowing with experienced and aggressive male photographers, many of whom had attended a Snake Dance at Walpi before. It was even more difficult for the Indians who danced with poisonous reptiles in the crowded conditions.

Behind Minna's camera was poised what she called the "acrobatic camera" of Ben Wittick who, according to one account, first began photographing the dances in the early 1880s. Wittick wrote to his wife that the 1897 Walpi dance was his sixth to attend. His large camera projected from a wall on an improvised platform, giving an unobstructed view of the ceremony but safely out of reach of any rattlesnakes. Wittick, who took his son Archie that year, wrote, "Such an awful crowd here . . . the Moqui Snake Dance is becoming more and more famous every succeeding year and they come from everywhere to see it." Fulfilling a prophecy made by Indians who opposed his photography, Wittick died in 1903 of a rattlesnake bite while attempting to package a snake to send to his Hopi friends for their dance. With stoicism the Indians commented, "Little Brother finally got him."[25]

Near Wittick's camera and in various other spots around the dance plaza were the cameras of Pasadena photographer Adam Clark Vroman. In his 1897 diary, Vroman complained that his "assistants" were so mesmerized by the dance they completely forgot their assigned duties, forcing him to jump from camera to camera, operating a total of seven by himself. One can only imagine the confusion Vroman caused as he darted from camera to camera, perhaps even across the plaza during the actual dance.

Without question the most aggressive of the California photographers was bearded George Wharton James, called "Big Black Bear" by the Havasupai Indians. With his large camera and tripod, James thought nothing of usurping a vital part of the compact dance plaza during the dance. A defrocked Methodist minister turned ethnologist-anthropologist, he published the first book about Grand Canyon in 1900 entitled, *In and Around the Grand Canyon*. He had on occasion forced his way into the Hopi Snake kiva (which is forbidden) and even boasted that just after the washing of the snakes for the dance, he made without the Indians' knowledge a time exposure of a "quiescent mass" of shiny reptiles intertwined on the kiva floor, some writhing from a hole in the kiva wall. Apparently, James feared neither the snakes nor the Hopis, who came to detest his pushiness. Though bitten by a rattlesnake in 1902, he did not die from the bite, perhaps because he wore a *klish* (snake) ring as immunity against poisonous snakebites; his Indian friends believed it had protected him from the venom.[26]

In Flagstaff earlier that summer, Jo Hollenback wrote of their concerns about photographing the Snake Dance:

> The subject of the possibility of being able to secure any photographs of the sight came up in the parlor [of the Bank Hotel] last night, when a number were talking about the Snake Dance. Opinions seemed to differ as to the advisability of attempting to photograph it at all, not alone on account of the lateness of the hour at which it occurs, five [six] o'clock in the afternoon, which time is as unalterable as the "laws of the Medes and Persians," and that would make it very difficult to secure a photograph on account of the light and the necessity of a time exposure, which the antics of the Indians would make impossible, but on account of the unwill-

ingness of the performers, themselves, who look upon the dance as a religious ceremony.

Very few photographs have ever been taken of the sight anyway; "one gentleman" here was of the opinion that none had been, but that was a mistake, for Professor James managed to get one or two, also Mr. Lummis, but it was the former who came near having a serious time with the Indians as a result of his persistent endeavors to photograph them, which they naturally resented as not in keeping with their idea of the sacredness of the event.[27]

After hearing the difficulty tales we all decided that it would be no photographs for us, unless they could be obtained without risk to anyone. . . .[28]

Minna, prudent as always, calculated the risk and decided to photograph the dance anyway. Nevertheless, while in Hopi she purchased twenty-one photographs of the Snake Dance from "Prof. James" for $6.88 and a dozen from "Mr. Wittick" for $8.00, for fear her own amateur efforts would fail.[29]

Apart from photographer and spectator behavior during the August 1897 dance, the sacred event might have taken on an even greater profanity later that same year. In July Albuquerque officials attempted to persuade the Hopis to dance it at the New Mexico Territorial Fair in September. Such a spectacular event would guarantee, in the opinion of fair officials, the largest crowd ever to attend the fair. Though the younger men at Hopi briefly entertained the proposal, the elders firmly declined.[30]

Spectators of the Snake Dance, meanwhile, provided a colorful show all their own. In 1903 George Wharton James described the scene: "The house-tops are lined with Hopis, Navahoes, Paiutis, cowboys, miners, Mormons, preachers, scientists and military men from Ft. Wingate and other western posts . . . a German savant and a representative of a leading scientific society of France." Add to the list prospectors, explorers, teachers, women, and children. Concerning the latter, James wrote, "To me the most interesting spectators . . . are the children. They have been long feasting on corn and melons, and the visitors who come to the dance generally bring a good supply of candy and other luxuries to the Moki 'menu.' The youngsters, therefore, are stuffed full and their little bellies become the most imposing portion of their makeup."[31]

While spectator behavior was uncontrollable, that of the snakes was unpredictable. At the 1897 ceremony one large snake slithered behind James and his camera; Wittick's camera caught the chaotic moment reflected in the faces of visitors and Indians alike. Dr. Fewkes wrote in his report that during the dance two large rattlesnakes became entwined, only to be "deftly disengaged" by one of the dancers. Scholar Walter Hough noted the immense size of the two snakes that almost succeeded in "breaking up the performance"; from their apparent age, these snakes might have been danced "around the ring before," he observed. Veteran dance observer Fewkes estimated two hundred non-Indian spectators, far too large for the very small Walpi plaza. Regarding the dancers, he wrote, "When gazed upon by so many strangers, some of the Snake men appeared to be more nervous, and did not handle the reptiles in the fearless manner which marked earlier performances."[32]

If Dr. Fewkes thought the dance that year was less than exciting, the Rev. Heinrich R. Voth, a Mennonite missionary on Third Mesa, later told Jo that "he never saw the Indians so excited, wrought up to the highest pitch, nor the snakes as fierce and angry as they were that day at Walpi." Like Fewkes, Voth had witnessed several other snake dances, keeping meticulous notes for the Field Columbian Museum in Chicago.[33]

Hopis are known not only as snake dancers but as fine runners as well. At dawn on the morning of the Snake Dance, a race is traditionally held. Running was a way of life, and the Indians thought nothing of running many miles to and from their fields in the course of a day. Thirty years later, in 1927 the New York-Long Beach Marathon (which began at the New York Athletic Club) became known as the Snake Dancer's Marathon when a Hopi Snake priest won the twenty-six-mile event.[34]

Though the two Snake priests may have received the most notice during the 1927 marathon, as they do during the Hopi Snake Dance, it is the Antelope priests who actually make all the preparations for the event. They are the first to enter the dance plaza to begin the sacred ceremony. On August 21, 1897, twelve Antelope priests moved from the Snake kiva, through a passageway among Walpi houses and took their places in a single line beside the kisi, eight adults on one side and four boys on the other. During the dance these small boys, perhaps six years of age, cautiously eyed any snake that came a little too close. The elderly Antelope chief, Wiki, a member of the Snake Clan of Walpi and uncle of the dashing Snake chief Kopeli, carried a flat rattle in his right hand. He also carried a basket tray of sacred cornmeal in his left, where the *tiponi*, the Antelope palladium or mantle of his position, rested. Painted white lines zigzagged his chest, back, arms, and legs. A small white feather clung to his hair. Wiki, a tall Hopi, wore a ceremonial kilt with a knotted sash, moccasins, and armlets; he knew the ceremony by heart, though he could not hear the singing. He could only feel the vibration of the drums because he was extremely deaf by 1897.[35]

Since the early 1890s, when ethnologists first began to study the Snake Dance, almost all of the older Antelope priests except Wiki had died. An unwritten heritage, Walpi snake lore had also died with these old Antelope priests. Dr. Fewkes, who researched and wrote extensively on the Hopis and their ceremonies, expressed this opinion in 1897; history eventually proved him correct in that the Snake Dance is no longer danced in Walpi. Vital snake lore disappeared in January 1899 with the death of Walpi's superb Snake priest Kopeli, who died of smallpox at age twenty-five after visiting Zuni Pueblo in New Mexico.[36]

Kopeli—son of Supela, one of the chiefs of the Patki (Rain-cloud people), and Saliko, the oldest woman of the Snake clan—had inherited his office as Snake chief from two uncles on his mother's side. Trader Thomas V. Keam, of nearby Keams Canyon, who it has been said knew the Walpi people better than any other white man, stated, "Kopeli was the best man of the Mokis . . . a *pac lolomai taka*, an excellent man, whose heart was good and whose speech was straight." Kopeli was considered a "friendly" not only because of his feeling for the whites but because he supported their innovations for the betterment of his people, such as education.[37]

Saliko, Kopeli's mother, was also influenced by the ways of the white man. She accepted their religion while in her seventies, refusing to prepare the medicine for the Snake Dance after she embraced Christianity. In 1897 Minna Hollenback photographed Saliko, calling her "The Lady of the House." She not only was that, but she owned the house. A matriarchal society, the Hopis believe that "the family, the dwelling house and the field are inseparable, because the woman is the heart of these, and they rest with her. Among us the family traces its kin from the mother, hence all its possessions are hers. The man builds the house but the woman is the owner, because she repairs and preserves it."[38]

A strong, devout woman, Saliko took to "The Faith" with a vengeance, her long and explicit prayers being among the loudest that went up from Hopi to the white man's God. When her husband Supela died, there wasn't a single missionary to be found at Hopi who could give him the burial she desired, even though her husband was not a Christian. But a traveling salesman was nearby who carried with him a black-bound book. Saliko convinced him to open his "black book" over her husband's grave, give a short sermon, and offer a prayer, in the belief that every black book was indeed a Bible.[39]

In August 1897, as the Antelope priests lined up on either side of the kisi facing east, the drumbeat changed in rhythm and intensity to announce the entrance of the Snake priests in all their splendor. Their faces and bodies were smeared with white and red paint, and wearing freshly painted snake kilts, the feathered Snake priests with their shell necklaces rattling dashed into the dance floor with primitive panache. The priests repeated the circling of the dance floor, passing the kisi on their right, dropping a pinch of cornmeal upon the sipapu and stamping on the plank.

The Antelope priests and the Snake priests then locked arms. To the rich, masculine singing of a melodious chant and the rattle of gourds, the two lines gently rocked to and fro, without the foot-stamping characteristic of the Kachina dance choreography of other Hopi ceremonials. After a time of rocking, the Snake priests divided into groups of three, each with a carrier, hugger, and gatherer, the names describing their functions. The carrier then knelt down before the kisi and retrieved a snake, venomous or otherwise, from the altar. With the writhing snake held by its neck in the dancer's mouth, its head pointed to the right, the carrier again circled the floor as the hugger deftly brushed the eagle feather in front of the snake's mouth to shield the carrier's face. The pair passed the sacred rock to the south (with spectators perched on top), where a row of women sprinkled the carrier with sacred cornmeal.

More than one photographer of the 1897 dance, including Minna Hollenback, showed Snake priests holding between their teeth tiny snakes whose heads reminded the viewer of a cigar in the dancers' mouths. Kopeli explained that snakes so small were not put in the kisi but were held in their mouths from the time they left the Snake kiva.[40]

Once all the snakes had been danced with, they were thrown into a circle in the center of the dance plaza, a prayer was repeated over them by Wiki, and they were again sprinkled with sacred meal. The Snake priests then quickly gathered up all their hands could hold and dashed down the foot trails to the four cardinal points, releasing their messengers of rain on the valley floor below.

Returning to the mesa top, the Snake priests went immediately to their kiva, removed all their dance paraphernalia, then gathered at the west side of the mesa, where they drank great quantities of emetic to induce vomiting. This purification ritual was followed with a feast for the hungry priests who had fasted all day. The Antelope priests quietly returned to their homes after undressing in their kiva. The sacred ceremonies continued in Hopi for several more, usually rainy days, without the scrutiny of strangers.

The subject of poisonous snakebites of the Snake priests is still hotly debated by ethnological authorities, with some claiming the emetic taken after the dance prevents poisoning or that the snakes have been defanged or their fangs milked. Some declare that the snakes have been sedated, while others postulate that they have simply grown tame after several years of use during the dance.

Much has been written about the treatment of snakes used in the dance. It has been said that the "feeling tone" of the Snake priests is not one of fear or repulsion toward the snakes, the animal patron of their cult. Reportedly, the poison sacs of the rattlesnake are removed before they are danced with, then they grow back, a "fact" that has been verified time and again; this would certainly lessen the fear of a dancer handling the poisonous reptile. There are other "verified" theories, and over the years the wily Hopis have used various and sundry methods of deceiving ethnologists and herpetologists, who have doggedly sought an answer to the snake poison mystery from as early as 1883.[41]

Once the Snake Dance ended in 1897, the many non-Indians abandoned the mesa in stunned silence to return to their own civilization, often amid a downpour of rain. None left, however, without a profound sense of having witnessed a ceremony from another world and another time. For the sisters the dance remained indelible in their memories. In 1972 José Ronquillo, the caretaker for thirty-six years of Amelia's Santa Fe house, was quick to inform the author, "You know, of course, she attended the Hopi Snake Dance before the turn of the century." Until the trunk with the letters and photographs from the 1897 trip was discovered in 1981, Ronquillo's statement held no significance.

Following their trip to Walpi, Minna and Jo returned to Flagstaff, and from there they revisited Laguna and Acoma. By September 4 they were in Albuquerque, leaving there on September 6th for Chicago and on to Glen Summit to join their family.

It is not known if Minna or Jo ever attended another Snake Dance at Hopi. Certainly, Amelia returned to the Southwest several times over the next thirty years. She returned west in 1905 with Dr. and Mrs. Louis Taylor, her sister and brother-in-law, traveling to Pike's Peak in Colorado and then to California. In 1906 she and "J" (Juliette) visited Grand Canyon, where they stayed at Fred Harvey's new El Tovar, opened the previous year. By the late 1920s Amelia apparently had resolved to return "out West" on a more permanent basis, and she contacted John Gaw Meem about building a home in Santa Fe in the Pueblo-revival architectural style. The seeds she and her sister had planted in 1897 would result in the fulfillment of her longtime connection to southwestern culture.

Hollenback Santa Fe residence. Author's collection.

The full story of how the house came to be, what she filled it with, and how the architect and the woman from Brooklyn collaborated in building it must wait for a future book. We do know that she had accumulated the necessary expertise by 1931-32 to present her knowledgeable vision of the house to Meem and to be an active partner in its construction. Finding the materials from the 1897 trip answered most of Meem's questions about how she acquired her knowledge and why she built it only to return to Brooklyn for most of the remaining thirty-seven years of her life. The pull of familiar surroundings and her beloved family, and the habits of her life in the East in general, were too strong to be resisted. The death in 1936 of her secretary and companion, Amalie Hoffmann, as well as World War II during the 1940s, surely played a key role. The "mystery" Meem challenged me to solve will continue to unfold as my research possibly reveals more clues about Amelia's seeming abandonment of her Santa Fe house.

Amelia's mother and father died in 1916 and 1923, respectively, and her beloved younger sister Juliette was gone by 1907. By 1905 Jo was married and living in Paris with her husband and baby son; a daughter arrived later—Dorothy, who would become Amelia's guardian in her last years.

While Minna and Jo may not have gained entrance to the Royal Geographical Society—or any other—for their 1897 Southwest adventures, their writings about the trip make a fascinating and valuable contribution to the history of early feminine tourism. And if and when other nineteenth-century photographs of the area by women are discovered, those of the Hollenbacks will remain significant to researchers of women's history in the Southwest.

In the fall of 1897 Minna Hollenback returned to Adelphi Academy in Brooklyn but soon dropped out, apparently too overwhelmed by the events of the summer to go back to her former routine. In recalling their adventures, no doubt she pitied all the "fat-wilted" persons referred to by Charles Lummis in his 1897 letter to her, the ones who never rode a mule to the bottom of Grand Canyon or who never fell under the mystical spell of Acoma. In the Keres language Acoma means "a place that always was"—an apt description of one encounter of Minna's immortal summer.

Notes

1. Hough, *Moki Snake Dance*, 24.

2. Adapted by A. M. Stephen from a version given to him by the Antelope chief, Wiki. Fewkes, Stephen, and Owens, "The Snake Ceremonials at Walpi," 106–19.

3. *Handbook of North American Indians*, 9:551; Sapir, "The Southern Paiute Language," 574.

4. Lyon, "History of Prohibition of Photography of Southwestern Indian Ceremonies." The public has been barred from the Mishongnovi Snake Dance on Second Mesa since 1986.

5. Kate Thompson Cory lived and photographed in Hopi from 1905 to 1912; her works are considered outstanding examples

of early southwestern photography. See Wright, Gaede, and Gaede, *The Hopi Photographs, Kate Cory*. In 1970 the Walpi Snake Society chief died, passing the office to his nephew who, because he felt unready, declined to do the dance in 1971. By 1973 the Antelope Society chief also had died, and his nephew declined to carry on the dance because he felt it should no longer be done. Kealiinohomoku to author, July 18, 1987.

6. The office and residence of Wilbur S. Robinson, M.D., was in the Presbyterian parsonage. *Flagstaff Sun-Democrat*, June 3, 1897. Silybum marianum (mariana mariana) was used at the turn of the century to treat menstrual symptoms, and cascara sagrada was a purgative. Wood and Bache, *Dispensatory*, 1439.

7. U.S. 1890 Census, HD 340, 186.

8. This is the first and only reference to Mr. Wilcox's heart problem.

9. Denis Riordan was the Navajo Indian agent in 1883, resigning in 1884 because of intolerable conditions at the agency. He then became superintendent of the Ayer Lumber Company in Flagstaff, where he purchased the Ayer interests in 1887. Timothy A. and Michael J. joined their brother in the lumber business, and along with F. W. Sisson, bought out D. M. Riordan in 1893. McNitt, *Indian Traders*, 58; Cline, *Mountain*, 162. According to the local newspaper, those in the Riordan party included the two sons of Aldace F. Walker of Chicago, new chairman of the board of directors of the Santa Fe Railway, and a party of young Chicagoans. *Flagstaff Sun-Democrat*, Aug. 12, 1897. Harry H. Hoxworth, born in Ohio in 1860, listed his occupation as a miner on the 1900 U.S. Census for Coconino County. He also owned H. H. Hoxworth & Company, a Flagstaff hardware store. Cline, *Mountain*, 228.

10. ABH to Juliette, July 22, 1897, finished July 28, HC. It is unclear which Mr. Clark Minna writes about. It may have been Elias S. Clark, a member of the Presbyterian Church, who in 1897 was Flagstaff's district attorney and later became Arizona's territorial attorney general. John and Asa Clark, for whom Clark Valley was named, were part of another early ranching and mercantile family in the Flagstaff area. Another Clark, Charley, accompanied New Jersey Congressman Charles N. Fowler and party to the Walpi Snake Dance. Cline, *Mountain*, 89, 152, 164; *Flagstaff Sun-Democrat*, Aug. 19, 1897. For more on John Francis, see n. 21 below.

11. Wittick to wife, Aug. 20, 1897, MNMHL, Santa Fe. Born in Huntingdon, Pa., Wittick first came to the Southwest around 1879 as an employee of the railroad. He established a studio in Albuquerque in 1881 and later, another in Gallup until 1900, when he moved to nearby Fort Wingate where he died. Rudisill, *Photographers of the New Mexico Territory*, 62–63. Wittick's negatives, glass lantern slides, and prints may be found in the Museum of New Mexico Photo Archives, Santa Fe; El Paso Centennial Museum; and Science Museum of Minnesota, St. Paul.

12. According to James E. Babbitt, Volz purchased the Canyon Diablo trading post from Pennsylvanian Charles H. Algert in 1897. In 1912 Volz sold his trading post at "The Fields" (about 32 miles from Canyon Diablo), established to accommodate his Snake Dance tours, to the Babbitt brothers, who remained there until 1922. It has been claimed that Frederick W. Volz witnessed more Snake Dances than any other white man. Babbitt, "Trading Posts," 4–5. Earlier in the summer, Minna had purchased provisions from the Babbitts in Flagstaff as well. ABH Expense diary, HC.

13. Hough, *Moki Snake Dance*, 55–59; Webb and Weinstein, *Dwellers*, 35; ABH Expense Diary, HC. Ethnologist Walter Hough attended the 1897 Walpi Snake Dance. McNitt, *Traders*, 270; Webb and Weinstein, *Dwellers*, 35. His Snake Dance book, published for tourists, included several of Vroman's 1897 photos that, had they not been cropped for publication, would have shown Amelia Hollenback with her camera.

See SAA, neg. no. 83-4200. See also MNMPA, neg. no. 2532 and SAA, neg. no. SPC 021689.00.

14. In the late 1890s Adam Clark Vroman also noted, "A heap of empty tins marks every halting place of the caravan." Webb and Weinstein, *Dwellers*, 35.

15. Yava, *Big Falling Snow*, 123, 161-64. Hamlin Garland wrote "The Iron Khiva," about these "iron-roofed" government houses. Underhill and Littlefield, Jr., *Garland*, 16.

16. H. James, *Pages from Hopi History*, 130-31. In 1890 Dr. Jesse Walter Fewkes first found only a few houses near the foot of First Mesa and on the surrounding plains, but by the turn of the century the number had increased substantially. Fewkes, "Tusayan Flute and Snake Ceremonies," 986 n. 1.

17. New Jersey Congressman Charles Newell Fowler and his son attended the 1897 Walpi Snake Dance. *Flagstaff Sun-Democrat*, Aug. 19, 1897.

18. Downum, *A Flagstaff Heritage*, 35-37.

19. Hockderffer, *Flagstaff Whoa!*, 119.

20. Downum, *Flagstaff Heritage*, 34; Hochderffer, *Flagstaff Whoa!*, 118. See also Corser, *Seventy-Six Page History of Alaska* and *Totem Lore of the Alaska Indians*. Born in 1864 at Portageville, N.Y., Corser attended LaFayette College in Easton, Pa., in 1885-1887 and Union Theological Seminary in 1896. He served at Fort Wrangell, Alaska, in the Presbyterian Church from 1900-1904, then, moving to the Episcopalians in 1905, he was in charge of St. Philip's Church there until he retired in 1934. He also organized the first Boy Scout troop in Alaska. Corser died in 1936. Robinson, *Directory*, 1:221; *Alaskan Churchman* (Feb. 1936), 10, AEC.

21. See Grey, *To the Last Man*. The 1923 Paramount movie based on Grey's novel was filmed near Payson and featured James Wong Howe as cameraman, with Richard Dix and Lois Wilson in the leads. It was directed by Victor Fleming of *Gone with the Wind* fame. After 1930 Grey never returned to Arizona, stating "The tourists were taking over the beauty spots and spoiling them with their refuse." Kant, *Zane Grey's Arizona*, 40, 49, 116, 140.

John William Francis, born in 1856 near Chillicothe, Mo., was an extraordinary lawman who held the fearful respect of many an outlaw. During one shoot-out, a fugitive stopped the confrontation and invited Francis and his deputy to breakfast. Well fed, the group again engaged in battle, with the ultimate killing of the morning's host. Cline, *Mountain*, 141.

22. Lawrence, *Mornings in Mexico*, 141.

23. Fewkes, "Tusayan Flute and Snake Ceremonies," 307.

24. Fewkes wrote that "it became a matter of grave concern to those who are familiar with the mode of construction of the walls and roofs of the pueblo whether they would support the great weight which they were called upon to bear. Happily these fears proved to be groundless, but if the spectators increase in number in the next presentations as rapidly as in the past, it will hardly be possible for the Pueblo to accommodate them." Fewkes, "Tusayan Flute and Snake Ceremonies," 978. Fewkes's assertion that fears regarding the possible collapse of mud roofs were groundless was wrong. One such death in 1855 was that of twenty-three-year-old Elias Spiegelberg of Santa Fe, N.M., a brother of five other Spiegelbergs, who were entrepreneurs and traders. Cook, "Flora Spiegelberg, "Tenderfoot Bride of the Santa Fe Trail," 11.

25. Minna's camera appears to be an 1897 No. 4 cartridge Kodak, which used roll film or glass plates; she used the latter. It is not clear if Wittick meant the sixth Snake Dance at Walpi only or that of other villages as well. Wittick to wife, Aug. 20, 1897, MNMHL; Packard and Packard, *Southwest 1880 with Ben Wittick*, 6. A newspaper account of his death relates that Wittick was trying to "tame" a rattlesnake. According to the paper,

the snakebite occurred around August 10. *Albuquerque Daily Citizen*, Sept. 1, 1903. This would have coincided with preparations for the Walpi Snake Dance in 1903, thus making plausible his packaging a snake for the Hopis when Wittick was bitten.

26. James, *Indians of the Painted Desert*, 114–17, 157 n. 1. See also Houlihan, "George Wharton James: Writer-Collector-Photographer."

27. The earliest photograph known of the Walpi Snake Dance appears to have been taken by Ben Wittick in 1883 (a photo identified by Lummis as "circa 1884," but the Snake Dance occurred in odd-numbered years only at Walpi). Lummis, *Mesa, Cañon and Pueblo*, 55. In the early 1880s Wittick first began to photograph the Hopi Snake Dance at Shongopavi. Van Valkenburgh, "Ben Wittick, Pioneer Photographer of the Southwest," 38. Albuquerque photographer W. Calvin Brown photographed the dance in 1885 (photos in private collection) and wrote a lengthy article about it. *Albuquerque Morning Journal*, Aug. 24, 1885.

28. JH to parents, July 2 to 4, 1897, HC.

29. Comparison of Minna's 1897 photographs of the Walpi Snake Dance with those of other known photographers indicates they were indeed her own and not ones purchased from James or Wittick, with the possible exception of one made from the dance rock area. The dance rock would have been across the dance floor from the spot where Amelia stood with her camera. The quality of the Hollenback photos, of course, does not match that of the professional photographers.

30. *Albuquerque Morning Democrat*, July 17, 1897. According to a rumor, the Hopis danced the Snake Dance in a New York penthouse ca. 1927.

31. James, *Indians of the Painted Desert*, 117; James Scrapbook, SM, Los Angeles. The protruding bellies of the children may have indicated malnutrition.

32. Fewkes, "Tusayan Flute and Snake Ceremonies," 978; Hough, *Moki Snake Dance*, 13. John G. Bourke, Washington Matthews, Maj. John Powell, and Adolph Bandelier all expressed opinions that Fewkes could not be trusted, but professional enmity among late-nineteenth-century ethnologists was more common than not. See Porter, *Paper Medicine Man*, 277–78.

33. Cushing, *Zuñi*, 30; JH to mother, Aug. 31, 1897, HC.

34. *New York Herald Tribune*, May 16, 1927, HC. Quanowahu was the name of the Snake priest; another Hopi, Pohoquaptewa, also ran the same race. In the 1912 Olympics held in Stockholm, Hopi runner Louis Tewanima won silver medals in both the 5,000- and 10,000-meter races of the pentathlon and the decathlon. Nabokov, *Indian Running*, 182.

35. Wiki had long wished to see a train moving along the railroad tracks that were a hundred miles or so south of Walpi. When he at last made the long journey to Holbrook, Arizona, the first thing he did was to walk along the tracks to wait for the train. Tragically, he failed to hear the warning whistle as it approached, and he was struck from behind and killed. Burbank, *Burbank among the Indians*, 94. Elbridge Ayer Burbank was the nephew of Mrs. Edward Ayer, for whom Ayer Point in Grand Canyon was named; he painted portraits of many important Hopis at the turn of the century.

36. For an early ethnographic account of the Walpi Snake Dance, see Bourke, *The Snake-Dance of the Moquis of Arizona*. An early published account (1893?) of it by a woman is that of Anna C. Egan, from Lawrence, Kans., who was the principal teacher at the Moqui Indian School at Keams Canyon, Arizona. Unidentified newspaper clipping in Welsh Murder File-1893, E. H. Plummer Papers, NMSA. For a brief eyewitness account of the 1898 Zuni smallpox epidemic and its spread to Hopi, see Yava, *Big Falling Snow*, 13.

37. Fewkes, "Death of a Celebrated Hopi," 196–97. In the fall of 1986, the author

attended a picnic near Walpi celebrating the opening of the first high school ever to be built on the Hopi Reservation, east of Walpi on the Keams Canyon road. At the picnic I heard discussions by Hopi elders of the importance of educating their children, while at the same time teaching them the ancient traditions of their ceremonial life. The question of conflict and balance between the two worlds remains paramount yet unanswerable.

38. Yava, *Big Falling Snow*, vii.

39. Means, *Sunlight on the Hopi Mesas*, 74–76.

40. Fewkes, "Tusayan Flute and Snake Ceremonies," 978.

41. Benedict, *Patterns of Culture*, 95. In 1883 two rattlesnakes were captured, sent to a museum in the East, and their fangs examined by Dr. S. Weir Mitchell of Philadelphia; the fangs were found undisturbed and the poison sacs intact and filled with venom. Mindeleff, "An Indian Snake Dance," 12–13. See also Klauber, "A Herpetological Review of the Hopi Snake Dance"; Bogert, "The Hopi Snake Dance," 276–83; Titiev, "Hopi Snake Handling," 44–51.

Bibliography

Abbreviations

AEC   Archives of the Episcopal Church

AHS   Arizona Historical Society

ASP   Arizona State Parks

CUA   Clark University Archives

CCR   Coconino County Records

FLM   Fort Leavenworth Museum

FVA   Fort Verde Archives

GCRL   Grand Canyon Research Library

HA   Heritage Associates

HC   Hollenback Collection

KSHS   Kansas State Historical Society

LCMNH   Los Angeles County Museum of Natural History

MCNML   Montezuma Castle National Monument Library

MNAL   Museum of Northern Arizona Library

MNMHL   Museum of New Mexico History Library

MNMPA   Museum of New Mexico Photo Archives

NPS   National Park Service

NMSA   New Mexico State Archives

SAA   Smithsonian Anthropological Archives

SM   Southwest Museum

Hollenback Collection

Hollenback Genealogy: Courtesy of Mrs. Virginia Welles, Wilkes-Barre, Pennsylvania.

Amelia B. Hollenback. Expense Diary, 1897.

———Journal, 1897.

———to Anna Hollenback. Grand Cañon Camp, undated [June 21, 1897]; Flagstaff, July 22, 1897.

———to Mabel Haddock. Grand Cañon Camp, undated [June 21, 1897].

———to mother. Flagstaff, June 13, 1897; undated note marked "Private; Grand Cañon Camp, July undated, to 5 and 10, 1897; Laguna and Gallup, to Flagstaff, July 30 to August 12, 1897.

———to Juliette Hollenback. Kansas City, Missouri, June 3, 1897; Fort Leavenworth, Kansas, to Flagstaff, June 4 to 10, 1897; Flagstaff, July 22, 1897 (Finished July 28).

Mrs. J. W. Hollenback to husband. Brooklyn, November 14 and December 17, 1897.

Josephine Hollenback to father. Flagstaff, June 10, 1897; Grand Cañon, June 27, 1897.

———to parents. Flagstaff, July 2 to 4, 1897; Flagstaff, to Laguna, August 31, 1897.

———to mother. Flagstaff, June 13, 1897.

———to Juliette Hollenback. Grand Cañon, June 20, 1897.

Claire G. Knox, proprietor of the Ideal Hotel, Flagstaff. Business card.

Charles F. Lummis to Amelia B. Hollenback. Los Angeles, May 18, 1897, cited in Josephine Hollenback to father, Brooklyn, May 23, 1897.

New York Herald Tribune. Clipping, May 16, 1927.

Archival Materials

Archives of the Episcopal Church, Austin, Texas.

    Alaskan Churchman (February 1936).

Arizona Historical Society, Tucson.

    Clipbook, John Hance. John Hance File.

    Manuscript Collection, John Hance's Visitor's Book.

    History File, John Hance.

Clark University Archives, Worcester, Massachusetts.

    William Libbey, Jr., Papers 1864–1905.

Fort Verde Archives, Camp Verde, Arizona.

    Altshuler File.

Grand Canyon Research Library, Arizona.

    Grand Canyon Study Collection.

    Bert Cameron, Grand Canyon Items, Vol. 2 (1886–1914).

    Frances Hance Rose to Lon Garrison, History File

Montezuma Castle National Monument Library, Verde Valley, Arizona.

    History Manuscript File.

Museum of New Mexico History Library, Santa Fe.

    Manuscript Collection, Ben Wittick.

Museum of New Mexico Photo Archives, Santa Fe.

    Mary Jane Colter Collection.

Museum of Northern Arizona Library, Flagstaff.

    Bright Angel Hotel Register.

    Mrs. Martin Buggeln Collection.

National Archives, Washington, D.C.

    Record Group 94. Compiled Service Records of Volunteer Union Soldiers Who Served in Organizations from the Territory of New Mexico.

New Mexico State Archives, Santa Fe.

    E. H. Plummer Papers.

Smithsonian Anthropological Archives, Washington, D.C.

    Letters Received, Bureau of Anthropology and Ethnology No.10 Collection.

Southwest Museum, Los Angeles.

    George Wharton James Scrapbook.

Correspondence

Donald Baird, Director, Museum of Natural History, Princeton University, Princeton, New Jersey, to author, September 18, 1984.

Author to Donald J. Orth, Santa Fe, New Mexico, October 20, 1984.

Robert C. Euler to author, December 27, 1987.

Larry Jochims, Kansas State Historical Society, Topeka, to author, August 27, 1982.

Joan Kealiinohomoku, Cross-Cultural Dance Resources, Flagstaff, to author, July 18, 1987.

Connie Menninger, Archivist of the Santa Fe Railway Archives, Kansas State Historical Society, Topeka, July 21, 1994.

Donald J. Orth, Executive Secretary for Domestic Geographic Names, United States Board on Geographic Names, Reston, Virginia, to author, July 25, 1985; April 29, 1987.

Richard Pinkerton, Chairman, Arizona State Geographic Names Board, Phoenix, to author, June 12, 1985.

Interviews

Elizabeth Twyeffort Drake, New York City, 1983.

Bernard Fontana, Tucson, Arizona, 1984.

Dorothy Twyeffort Hubbell, Bedford, New York, 1982.

Maria Martinez and Blue Corn Calabaza, San Ildefonso, New Mexico, 1980–1982.

José Ronquillo, Santa Fe, New Mexico, 1972.

Paul Webb, Verde Valley, Arizona, 1985.

Newspapers

Albuquerque Daily Citizen

Albuquerque Morning Democrat

Albuquerque Morning Journal

Albuquerque Weekly Citizen

Albuquerque Weekly Journal

Arizona Champion, Flagstaff

Arizona Enterprise, Tucson

Arizona Republic, Phoenix

Arizona Weekly Journal-Miner, Prescott

Flagstaff Coconino Sun

Flagstaff Gem

Flagstaff Sun-Democrat

Hartford Courant

Los Angeles Daily Times

New York Times

New York Herald Tribune

Princeton News

San Francisco Chronicle

Unpublished Sources

Arizona State Parks, Phoenix.

    Arizona State Inventory of Historic Places, Coconino County.

Coconino County Records, Flagstaff.

    Deed Books 2 and 32.

    Homestead Records Index.

Heritage Associates, Inc., Albuquerque.

    W. W. Bass Collection.

Lyon, Luke. "History of Prohibition of Photography of Southwestern Indian Ceremonies." Paper presented at a conference on Researching Dance Through Film and Video, sponsored by the Congress on Research in Dance and the Human Studies Film Archives, Smithsonian Institution, Washington, D.C., April 12, 1986.

Madsen, Lisa D. "The Grand Canyon Tourist Business of the W. W. Bass Family." Master's thesis, University of New Mexico, 1980.

National Register of Historic Places. Inventory-Nomination Form, Bank Hotel, May 2, 1977, and Fern Mountain, October 27, 1977.

Sarsfield, Luke Aloysius. "Matthias Hollenback: Early Wyoming Valley Entrepreneur." Ph.D. diss., New York University, 1973.

Printed Sources

Appletons' Cyclopaedia of American Biography. Vol. 4. Ed. James Grant Wilson. New York: D. Appleton, 1887–1900.

Babbitt, James E. "Trading Posts along the Little Colorado River." *Plateau Magazine of the Museum of Northern Arizona* 57, no. 3 (1986).

Barnes, Will C. *Arizona Place Names*, Rev. ed. Ed. Byrd H. Granger. Tucson: University of Arizona Press, 1982.

Bartlett, Katherine. "Notes upon the Routes of Espejo and Farfán to the Mines in the Sixteenth Century." *New Mexico Historical Review* 17, no. 1 (January 1942).

Benedict, Ruth. *Patterns of Culture*. Boston: Houghton Mifflin Company, 1934.

Billingsley, George H. "Prospector's Proving Ground: Mining in the Grand Canyon." *Journal of Arizona History* 17, no. 1 (spring 1976).

Bird, Isabella L. *A Lady's Life in the Rocky Mountains*. 1879. Reprint, Norman: University of Oklahoma Press, 1960.

Bloom, Lansing, ed. "Bourke on the Southwest." *New Mexico Historical Review*

12, no. 4 (October 1937).

Bogert, C. M. "The Hopi Snake Dance." *Natural History* (May 1941).

Bourke, John G. *The Snake-Dance of the Moquis of Arizona*. New York: Charles Scribner's Sons, 1884.

Bunting, Bainbridge. *John Gaw Meem: Southwestern Architect*. Albuquerque: University of New Mexico Press, 1983.

Burbank, E. A. *Burbank among the Indians*. Caldwell, Idaho: Caxton Printers, Ltd., 1944.

Carter, William Harding. *The Life of Lieutenant General Chaffee*. Chicago: University of Chicago Press, 1917.

Cline, Platt. *They Came to the Mountain*. Flagstaff, Ariz.: Northland Press, 1976.

Coble, C. H., and W. H. Power Map. *The Land of Sunshine* 7 (June–November 1897).

Colton, Harold Sellers. *The Sinagua: A Summary of the Archaeology of the Region of Flagstaff, Arizona*. Flagstaff: Northern Arizona Society of Science and Art, June 1946.

Cook, Mary Jean. "Flora Spiegelberg, Tenderfoot Bride of the Santa Fe Trail." *Wagon Tracks* (November 2000).

Corser, Harry P. *Seventy-Six Page History of Alaska*. N.p., ca. 1927.

———. *Totem Lore of the Alaska Indians*. Juneau: Nugget Shop, ca. 1930.

Cushing, Frank Hamilton. *Zuñi*. Ed. Jesse Green. Lincoln: University of Nebraska Press, 1979.

Dictionary of American Biography. Vol. 3. New York: Charles Scribner's Sons, 1929.

Downum, Garland. *A Flagstaff Heritage: The Federated Community Church*. Flagstaff, Ariz.: Federated Community Church, 1983.

Fewkes, Jesse Walter. "Death of a Celebrated Hopi." *American Anthropologist* 1, no. 1 (January 1899).

———. "Tusayan Snake Ceremonies." *Sixteenth Annual Report of the Bureau of American Ethnology 1894–95*. Washington, D.C.: Government Printing Office, 1897.

———. "Tusayan Flute and Snake Ceremonies." *Nineteenth Annual Report of the Bureau of American Ethnology (1897–98)*. Part 2. Washington, D.C.: Government Printing Office, 1900.

Fewkes, Jesse Walter, A. M. Stephen, and J. G. Owens. "The Snake Ceremonials at Walpi." *Journal of American Ethnology and Archaeology* 4 (1894).

Fiske, Turbese, and Keith Lummis. *Charles F. Lummis: The Man and His West*. Norman: University of Oklahoma Press, 1975.

Frazer, Robert W. *Forts of the West*. Norman: University of Oklahoma Press, 1965.

From Train to Plane: Travelers in the American West 1866–1936. Brochure for an exhibition in the Beinecke Rare Book and Manuscript Library. Entry no. 46. New Haven, Conn.: Yale University, 1979.

Garland, Hamlin. "A Day at Zuni." In Lonnie E. Underhill and Daniel F. Littlefield, Jr., *Hamlin Garland's Observations on the American Indian 1895–1905*. Tucson: University of Arizona Press, 1976.

———. *The Captain of the Gray-Horse Troop*. New York: Harper and Brothers, 1902.

———. "The Iron Khiva." *Harper's Weekly*, August 1903.

Grant, Bruce. *American Forts Yesterday and Today*. New York: E. P. Dutton and Co., Inc., 1965.

Grattan, Virginia L. *Mary Colter: Builder upon the Red Earth*. Flagstaff, Ariz.: Northland Press, 1980.

Grey, Zane. *To the Last Man*. 1922. Reprint, New York: Grosset, 1976.

Hall, Sharlot. "How I Saw the Grand Canyon of the Colorado at Midnight." *Travel* 2 (September 1897).

Harvey, Oscar Jewell, and Ernest Gray

Smith. *A History of Wilkes-Barre, Luzerne County, Pennsylvania*. Vol. 5. Wilkes-Barre: Raeder Press, 1909–1930.

Harwood, Herbert H., Jr. "Corporate History of the Lehigh Valley R.R." Bulletin no. 126. Boston: Railway and Locomotive Historical Society, 1972.

Hayes, Alden C. *The Four Churches of Pecos*. Albuquerque: University of New Mexico Press, 1974.

Heitman, Francis B. *Historical Register and Dictionary of the United States Army*. Vol. 1. Washington, D.C.: Government Printing Office, 1903.

Higgins, C. A. *Titan of Chasms: The Grand Canyon of Arizona*. Chicago: Santa Fe Railroad, 1906.

Hockderffer, George. *Flagstaff Whoa!* Flagstaff: Museum of Northern Arizona, 1965.

Hodge, Frederick Webb. "Katzimo the Enchanted." *Land of Sunshine* 7, no. 6 (November 1897).

Holmes, Burton. *The Burton Holmes Travelogues*. Vol. 12. Chicago: The Travelogue Bureau, 1920.

Hough, Walter. *The Moki Snake Dance*. Chicago: Santa Fe Railroad, 1898.

Houlihan, Patrick T. "George Wharton James: Writer-Collector-Photographer." *Masterkey* 60, no. 1 (spring 1986).

Hughes, J. Donald. *In the House of Stone and Light*. Grand Canyon, Ariz.: Grand Canyon Natural History Association, 1978.

Hunt, Elvid. *History of Fort Leavenworth 1827–1937*. 1937. Reprint, Fort Leavenworth, Kans.: Command and General Staff School Press, 1981.

James, George Wharton. *The Grand Canyon of Arizona: How to See It*. Boston: Little, Brown and Company, 1910.

———. *In and Around the Grand Canyon*. Boston: Little, Brown and Company, 1900.

———. *Indians of the Painted Desert*. Boston: Little, Brown and Company, 1905.

James, Harry C. *Pages from Hopi History*. Tucson: University of Arizona Press, 1979.

Kant, Candace C. *Zane Grey's Arizona*. Flagstaff, Ariz.: Northland Press, 1984.

Kessell, John. *The Missions of New Mexico Since 1776*. Albuquerque: University of New Mexico Press, 1980.

Klauber, L. M. "A Herpetological Review of the Hopi Snake Dance." *Bulletins of the Zoological Society of San Diego* (January 1932).

Knight, Oliver. *Life and Manners in the Frontier Army*. Norman: University of Oklahoma Press, 1978.

Lawrence, D. H. *Mornings in Mexico*. New York: Alfred A. Knopf, 1927.

Leavengood, Betty. *Grand Canyon Women: Lives Shaped by Landscape*. Boulder, Colo.: Pruett Publishing Company, 1999.

Leavenworth County Museum. Brochure. Leavenworth, Kans.: Leavenworth County Historical Society, n.d.

Lockwood, Frank C. *The Life of Edward E. Ayer*. Chicago: A. C. McClurg and Company, 1929.

Lowe, Percival G. *Five Years a Dragoon*. Norman: University of Oklahoma Press, 1965.

Lowell, Percival. *Mars*. Boston: Houghton, Mifflin and Co., 1895.

Lummis, Charles F. "The Disenchanted Libbey." *Land of Sunshine* 7, no. 5 (October 1897).

———. "Flagstaff, Arizona." *Land of Sunshine* 4 (December 1895–May 1896).

———. *The Land of Poco Tiempo*. New York: The Century Co., 1893.

———. *Mesa, Cañon and Pueblo*. 1925. Reprint, New York: D. Appleton-Century Company, 1938.

———. "The Rescue of Montezuma's Castle." *Land of Sunshine* 10 (December 1898–May 1899).

———. *Some Strange Corners of Our Country*. New York: The Century Co., 1892.

———. *The Spanish Pioneers*. Chicago: A. C. McClurg and Co., 1893.

———. "Three Weeks in Wonderland." *Land of Sunshine* 9, no. 3 (August 1898).

———. *A Tramp across the Continent*. 1892. Reprint, Lincoln: University of Nebraska Press, 1982.

———. "A Week of Wonders." *Out West* 16, no. 1 (January 1902).

Mahood, Ruth I., ed. *Photographer of the Southwest: Adam Clark Vroman 1856-1916*. Los Angeles: Ward Ritchie Press, 1961.

Mangum, Richard and Sherry. *Grand Canyon-Flagstaff Stage Coach Line*. Flagstaff, Ariz.: Hexagon Press, Inc., 1999.

Marshall, James. *Santa Fe: The Railroad That Built an Empire*. New York: Random House, 1945.

Maurer, Stephen G., ed. *Grand Canyon by Stage*. Albuquerque: Heritage Associates, 1982.

McCroskey, Mona Lange, ed. *Summer Sojourn to the Grand Canyon: The 1898 Diary of Zella Dysart*. Prescott, Ariz.: HollyBear Press, 1996.

McGehee, Micajah. "Rough Times in Rough Places." *Century Magazine* 41 (March 1891).

McNitt, Frank. *The Indian Traders*. Norman: University of Oklahoma Press, 1962.

Means, Florence Crannell. *Sunlight on the Hopi Mesas: The Story of Abigail E. Johnson*. Philadelphia: Judson Press, 1960.

Mearns, Edgar A. "Ancient Dwellings of the Rio Verde Valley." *Popular Science Monthly* 37 (May–October 1890).

Miller, Joshua A. "Montezuma Castle Repair Expedition." *Antiquarian* 1 (September 1897).

Mindeleff, Cosmos. "An Indian Snake Dance." *Science: An Illustrated Journal* 8 (July–December 1886).

Minge, Ward Alan. *Acoma: Pueblo in the Sky*. Albuquerque: University of New Mexico Press, 1976.

Montezuma Castle Trail Guide. Globe, Ariz: Southwest Parks and Monuments Association., n.d.

Myers, Wilbur A., and Edward Hanlon. *Historical Album of Wilkes-Barre and Wyoming Valley in Luzerne County, Pennsylvania 1729 to 1976*. Wilkes-Barre: Luzerne County Bicentennial Commission, 1976.

Nabokov, Peter. *Indian Running*. Santa Barbara, Calif.: Capra Press, 1981.

Nentvig, Juan, S.J. *Rudo Ensayo*. Tucson: University of Arizona Press, 1980.

Niven, John. *Gideon Welles: Lincoln's Secretary of the Navy*. New York: Oxford University Press, 1973.

Ortiz, Alfonso, ed. *Handbook of North American Indians*. Vol. 9. Washington, D.C.: Smithsonian Institution Press, 1979.

Packard, Gar, and Maggy Packard. *Southwest 1880 with Ben Wittick, Pioneer Photographer of Indian and Frontier Life*. Santa Fe, N. Mex.: Packard Publications, 1970.

Parish, William J. Errata of "The German Jew and the Commercial Revolution in Territorial New Mexico." *New Mexico Historical Review* 35, no. 2 (April 1960).

Pattee, C. R. "Flagstaff and the Grand Canyon." *Land of Sunshine* 7 (June–November 1897).

Porter, Joseph C. *Paper Medicine Man: John Gregory Bourke and His American West*. Norman: University of Oklahoma Press, 1986.

Powell, H. Benjamin. *Philadelphia's First Fuel Crisis: Jacob Cist and the Developing Market for Pennsylvania Anthracite*. University Park: Pennsylvania State University Press, 1978.

Prucha, Francis Paul. *A Guide to the Military Posts of the United States 1789-1895*. Madison: State Historical Society of Wisconsin, 1964.

Quebbeman, Frances E. *Medicine in Territorial Arizona*. Phoenix: Arizona Historical Foundation, 1966.

Robinson, Edgar Sutton, ed. *The Presbyterian Ministerial Directory (Northern)*. Vol. 1. Oxford, Ohio: Ministerial Directory Co., 1898.

Rudisill, Richard, comp. *Photographers of the New Mexico Territory 1854–1912*. Santa Fe: Museum of New Mexico, 1973.

Sandburg, Carl. *Abraham Lincoln*. 5 vols. New York: Charles Scribner's Sons, 1926–1939.

Sapir, Edward. "The Southern Paiute Language." *Proceedings of the American Academy of Arts and Sciences* 65, no. 1 (June 1930).

Schroeder, Albert H., and Homer F. Hastings. *Montezuma Castle National Monument*. National Park Service Historical Handbook Series no. 27. 1958. Reprint, Washington, D.C.: National Park Service, 1961.

Simmons, Marc. *Following the Santa Fe Trail*. Rev. ed. Santa Fe, N. Mex.: Ancient City Press, 1986.

Stanton, Robert Brewster. *Down the Colorado*. Norman: University of Oklahoma Press, 1965.

Thrapp, Dan L. *The Conquest of Apacheria*. Norman: University of Oklahoma Press, 1964.

Titiev, Mischa. "Hopi Snake Handling." *Scientific Monthly* 57 (July 1943).

University of Arizona Bulletin 6, no. 2 (January 1935).

U.S. Bureau of Census.

    1870 Decennial, Arizona Territory.

    1890 Census in House Doc. 340 (Part 15), 52d Cong., 1st sess. Washington, D.C.: Government Printing Office, 1894.

    1900 New Mexico Territory, Valencia County.

    1900 Arizona Territory.

U.S. Department of the Interior. *Annual Report of the Commissioner of Indian Affairs, 1882*. Washington, D.C.: Government Printing Office, 1882.

———. *Annual Report of the Commissioner of Indian Affairs for the Fiscal Year Ended June 30, 1898*. Washington, D.C.: Government Printing Office, 1898.

U.S. Secretary of War. *Annual Report 1897*. Washington, D.C.: Government Printing Office, 1897.

Van Valkenburgh, Richard. "Ben Wittick, Pioneer Photographer of the Southwest." *Arizona Highways* 18, no. 8 (August 1942).

Wahmann, Russell. "Grand Canyon Stage Line." *Desert Magazine* (January 1975).

Webb, George Ernest. *Tree Rings and Telescopes: The Scientific Career of A. E. Douglass*. Tucson: University of Arizona Press, 1983.

Webb, William, and Robert A. Weinstein. *Dwellers at the Source*. New York: Grossman Publishers, 1973.

Wellmann, Klaus F. *North American Indian Rock Art*. Graz, Austria: Akademische Druck-u. Verlagsanstalt, 1979.

Wells, H. G. *The War of the Worlds*. London: William Heinemann, 1898.

Wetmore, Helen Cody. *Last of the Great Scouts*. Chicago: Duluth Press Publishing Company, 1899.

Whitney, Stephen. *A Field Guide to the Grand Canyon*. New York: Quill, 1982.

Wilkins, Thurman. *Thomas Moran: Artist of the Mountains*. Norman: University of Oklahoma Press, 1966.

Wise, Hugh D. "Experiments with Kites." *Century Magazine* 54 (May 1897).

Wood, George B., and Franklin Bache. *Dispensatory of the United States of America*. 19th ed. Philadelphia: J. B. Lippincott Company, 1907.

Woods, G. K., ed. *Personal Impressions of the Grand Cañon of the Colorado River Near Flagstaff, Arizona, as Seen Through Nearly Two Thousand Eyes, and Written in the Private Visitors' Book of the World-Famous Guide Capt. John Hance*. San Francisco: Whitaker & Ray Company, 1899.

Wright, Barton, Marnie Gaede, and Marc Gaede. *The Hopi Photographs, Kate Cory: 1905–1912*. La Cañada, Calif.: Chaco Press, 1986.

Yava, Albert. *Big Falling Snow*. Albuquerque: University of New Mexico Press, 1978.

Zetland (Earl of Ronaldshay), Lawrence John Lumley Dundas. *The Life of Lord Curzon*. Vol. 1. London: E. Benn, Ltd., 1928.

Index

Acoma Pueblo, N. M., *Katzimo* (Enchanted Mesa), 8, 113, 116–117, 119–121, 123–24, 125–26, 129 n. 14, **photos of, 87-92**; ascent by William Libbey, Jr., 117, 120; ascent by Frederick W. Hodge, 113, 116–117.
Adelphi Academy (Brooklyn), 2, 9, 11, 146.
Ahnawita, (First Mesa), 136.
Antelope Dance (Corn Dance), 139.
Atlantic & Pacific Railroad (Santa Fe Pacific), 22–23, 44, 62, 113.
Ayer, Emma Augusta Burbank (Mrs. Edward E.), 20, 59, 72 n. 1, 74 n. 12.

Babbitt Brothers Trading Company (see East Cedar Ranch).
Bank Hotel (New), 56 n. 3.
Bass, Ada Diefendorf (Mrs. William Wallace), 60.
Beard, Amelia (see Amelia Beard Hollenback).
Beard, Anna Elizabeth (see Anna Elizabeth Beard Hollenback).
Beard, Eli, 129 n. 20.
Bercovitz, Rev. and Mrs. Moses, 119, 122–23, 129 n. 12, **photo of, 92**; Nathaniel, **photo of, 87**.
Bibo, Solomon (see Juana Valle).
Big Burro Springs (Ariz.), 136, 137, **photo of, 95**.
Bissell Point (see also Zuni Point), 54, 61, 63, 65, 74 n. 12.
Black Diamond Express (Lehigh Valley Railroad), 9, 12, 19 n. 2.
Bourke, Capt. John Gregory, 113.
Bridgeman, Herbert L, Brooklyn newspaperman, 134–135.
Brooklyn, N.Y., (see Hollenback family).
Brown, W. Calvin, photographer, 20 n. 13.

Bugglen, Martin and Mrs. Eva, 57 n.9.

Calabaza, Blue Corn (San Ildefonso potter), 73 n. 7, **photo of, 5**.
California Limited (Santa Fe Railway), 12.
Cameron, Annie, 59.
Cameron Trail (Grand View), 55.
Cañon or canyon, spelling of, 40 n. 4, 58 n. 18.
Carpio, Manuel, and Felicita, 7, 8 n. 9.
Chaffee, Col. Adna Romanza, 15, 104, 115; battle of Big Dry Wash and Gray Horse Troop, 21 n. 15.
Cist, Jacob (see also Hollenback family), 19 n. 4.
Clark, Mr., 134. 147 n. 10.
Clayton, Mr., general manager, 49, 68.
Colorado River (Grand Canyon), **photo of, 82**.
Colter, Mary Jane, architect, 111 n. 5.
Corser, Rev. Harry Prosper, 22, 27, 31, 33, 38–39, 71, 118, 137–38, 148 n. 20.
Cory, Kate Thompson, photographer, 146 n. 5.
Curzon of Kedleston, Lord, 1.

Davis, John, driver, 120, **photo of, 87**.
Denis, Misses Fannie J. and Ella P., matrons at Zuni school, 129; **photo of, 93**.
Docher, Rev. Antonine, 7, 8 n. 9.
Douglass, Andrew Ellicott (see Lowell Observatory).
Dox, Virginia (Dox Castle), 59, 72 n. 4.
Doyle, Sarah Allen, 59.
Drake, Elizabeth Twyeffort, viii.
Dutton, Mrs. and Mrs. A. A., 59.

East Cedar Ranch (Ariz.), 44, 56 n. 5.

159

Eddy, Charles Bishop, 128 n. 4.
Egan, Anna C., schoolteacher, 149 n. 36.

Ferguson, Josephine Woodward (see Josephine W. F. Hollenback).
Fewkes, Jesse Walter, ethnologist, 139, 141–42, 148 n. 24, 149 n. 32.
Finnie house (Verde Valley, Ariz.), 104, 107–09, 112 n. 14, **photo of Soda Spring, 86**.
Flagstaff (Ariz.), 49, **photos of, 76, 77**.
Fort Leavenworth, Kans., 9, 20 n. 10, 20 n. 12, **photos of, 75**; Soldiers' Home, 16, 21 n. 16, 20 n. 17; prison, 21 n. 17.
Fort Riley, Kans., 18, 21 n. 18.
Francis, John W., sheriff, 134, 137–138, 148 n. 21, **photo of, 96**.

Glen Summit, Pa. (see Hollenback family).
Graham, Douglas D., Indian trader, 119, 124, 129 n. 13; **photo of, 93**.
Grand Canyon (Ariz.) 119, **photos of, 80–85**.

Haddock, Mabel, 10, 44.
Hall, Sharlot, historian, 59.
Hance, John, guide, 43, 46–47, 48, 50, 52, 54, 55, 57 n. 9, 58 n. 10, 58 n. 15, 59, 63, 65–68, 72, 73 n. 8, 74 n. 12, **photo of, and house, 78**; New Hance Trail (Red Canyon), 49, 57, **photo of old trail, 82**; and Gen. Custer, 46, 53, 58 n. 17.
Hanna, Adam (Adamana named for), 8 n. 9, 62.
Harvey, Fred Company, 22, 23; El Tovar (hotel), 22.
Hawkins, Col. Hamilton S., K.O., 15, 21 n. 14.
Hoffmann, Amalie, secretary, 146; **photo of, 5**.
Hollenback, Amelia Beard (Minna), 1, 4, and Indians 60; Santa Fe, N.M. house, xii, **photo of; 145**; photos of Amelia, ii, xii, 3, 5, 78–79, 81–83, 87–88, 96, 100. Letters from: Kansas City, Mo., 12–13; Fort Leavenworth, Kans., 13–15; Acoma, N.M., 119–23; Flagstaff, Ariz., 15–18, 24–30, 37–40, 63–64, 70–72, 104–10, 125–27, 133–35; Gallup, N.M., 122–24; Grand Canyon, Ariz., 44–51, 68–69; Laguna,

N.M., 119–122. Floors of Montezuma Castle, 102.
Hollenback, Amelia Beard (3rd wife of J. W. Hollenback), 3–5, 9, 128 n. 4.
Hollenback, Anna (Nan), 5, 12.
Hollenback, Anna Elizabeth Beard, 1st wife of J. W. Hollenback, 3.
Hollenback Collection, vii–xi.
Hollenback, Eleanor Jones, wife of C.F. Welles, 3.
Hollenback family, 3, 10, 11, 19; genealogy, 3–4; Brooklyn residence, vii, 2, 13, **photo of, 6**; Glen Summit, Pa., 3, 10, 24, 30, 36, 45, 47, 62, 126–127, **photo of, vi**; cemetery, ix.
Hollenback, George, 4.
Hollenback, John Welles, ix, 2–4, 11, 60, 128 n. 4.
Hollenback, Josephine Woodward, daughter of J. W. Hollenback, 1, 146; **photos of, xii, 2, 79, 88**; letters from: Acoma, N.M., 118–19; Flagstaff, Ariz., 30–37, 65–68, 114–116, 140–41; from Grand Canyon, 51–55, 61–63, 65–68.
Hollenback, Josephine Woodward Ferguson, 2nd wife of J. W. Hollenback, 3, 11.
Hollenback, Juliette, daughter of J. W. Hollenback, 9, 11, 13–15, 51, 145.
Hollenback, Matthias, entrepreneur, x, 19 n.4.
Hollenback Point (Papago Point), Grand Canyon, Ariz., 43, 64, 67–68, 73 n. 11.
Hollenback sisters: Emily, Eleanor, Anna, Josephine, Amelia, and Juliette, 1.
Honani, Hopi Chief of Shungopavi, 136.
Hopi, 132; **photos of, 95–98, Moqui maiden, 100**.
Hough, Walter, ethnologist, 141, 147 n. 13.
Hoxworth, W. W., 133, 147 n. 9.
Hubbell, Dorothy Twyeffort, viii.

Isleta Pueblo, N. M., 8.

James, George Wharton, photographer, 74 n. 12, 132, 140–141.

Keam, Thomas V., Indian trader, 143.
Kipp, Dr., 31.
Kirsch, Math and Piedad, 5, 8 n. 9.
Knox, Mrs. W. H. and Miss Knox, 31–32, 34,

35–37, 41 n. 12, 71, 72, 105, 107.
Kopeli, Walpi Snake priest, 143.

Laguna Pueblo, N.M., 8 n. 9, 110, 113, 118–119, **photos of**, **92**.
La Junta, Colo., 114.
Lawrence, D. H., author, 138.
Libbey, William Jr., (see also Acoma) 64, 110, 111, 118, 125, 128 n. 8, 128 n. 10, 134–135.
Lightfoot, Dr., 59.
Lololomai (Old Oraibi, Third Mesa), 136.
Lummis, Charles F., 5–6, 7 n. 8, 21 n. 15, 30, 40 n. 6, 41, 58 n. 11, 113, 116–118, 128 n. 8, 141.
Lowell Observatory (Flagstaff), Percival Lowell and Andrew Endicott Douglass, 23, 32–33, 41 n. 15.
Lucero, gov. of Zuni, **photo of**, **93**.

McElderry, Maj. Henry, fort physician, 16–17.
Martínez, María (San Ildefonso potter), 73 n. 7, **photo of**, **5**.
Maude, Frederick Hamer, photographer, 132.
Mearns, Dr. Edgar A., 103, 112 n. 8.
Meem, John Gaw, architect, vii–viii, ix, xi n. 1, 24, 111 n. 5, 145–146.
Miller, Dr. Joshua A., 101–02, 111 n. 2, 111 n. 6.
Miner, Maj., 59.
Monsen, Frederick Hamer, photographer, 132.
Montezuma Well & Castle (Ariz.), 7, 7 n. 3, 8 n. 9, 26–27, 40 n. 6, 72, 101–03, 105, 108–09, 110, 111 n. 1, 111 n. 6; **photos of**, **85, 86**.
Moran Point (Grand Canyon), 50, 55, 58 n. 20, 61, 74 n. 12.
Mules, Kitty and Fatty, and horses (at Grand Canyon), 47, 52–53, 55, **photo of**, **79**.

Natural Bridge (Tonto Natural Bridge State Park), 7, 8 n. 9, 31, 40 n. 7.
Northern Arizona Normal School (Northern Arizona University), 40 n. 8.

Olney, Florence (schoolteacher), 37–39, 41 n. 18, 108, 134, 136–37, 138, **photo of**, **96**.

Oregon Trail, 20 n. 10.

Palakiki (govt. houses at Hopi), 136, 148 n. 16.
Papago Point (see Hollenback Point).
Pecos Pueblo ruins, 116, 128 n. 6.
Petrified Forest, 62, **photo of**, **76**.

Reid, Frank C., 40, 41, 101, 137, **photo of**, **96**.
Riordan, D.M., M.J., and T.A. (brothers), 133–34, 147 n. 9.
Robinson, Dr. Wilbur S., 132, 147 n. 6.
Ronquillo, José, caretaker of Santa Fe house, ix–xi, xi n. 2, 145.

Saliko, mother of Kopeli, 143.
San Ildefonso Pueblo Indians, 60, **photo of**, **5**.
Santa Fe Trail, 113.
Second Mesa (Hopi), **photo of sisters**, **97**.
See, T. J. J., 32.
Sibley, Henry Hopkins, 44, 56 n. 6.
Sichumovi, Hopi village, **photos of**, **96**.
Simo, (First Mesa), 136.
Sipapu, 60.
Sisson, Mary Willcox (Mrs. Frederick), 24–25, 31, 35, 40 n. 5.
Snake Dance (Hopi), 29, 62, 130, 132, 139–40, 141, 144, 147 n. 5, 150 n. 41, **photo of**, **99**.
Snake Dancer's Marathon, Quanowahu, 142; Pohoquaptewa and 1912 Olympics, 149 n. 34.
Snake Legend (Hopi), 130–32.
Stagecoaches, to South Rim, 45, 56 n. 4, 57 n. 7.
Stanton, Gen. and Mrs. Henry, 15, 20 n. 13.
Stanton, Robert Brewster, 60.
Starvation Peak (N.M.), 116, **photo of**, **76**.
Stevens, Lt. And Mrs. Charles Josiah Stevens (Ninth Cavalry), 14–15, 17, 19 n. 3, 20 n. 11, 20 n. 12, **photo of**, **75**.
Straw, Mary J., tombstone of, x.
Sturgis, Miss, 59.
Sunset Mountain and Crater (Ariz.), 37–39, 41 n. 19, 42 n. 21, 42 n. 22.
Supela, father of Kopeli.

Tesuque Pueblo Indians, **photo of**, **6**.

Thurber, Baby Grace and Lotty, **photos of**, **79**, **82**.
Thurber, J. Wilbur and Mrs. (Grand Canyon Stage Line), 44, 60, 134, 137, **photo of**, **96**.
Thurber's Camp, 48; history of, 57 n. 9, **photos of**, **77**, **78**.
Tolfree, J. L. (proprietor, New Bank Hotel), 28, 44.

Valle, Juana (Acoma wife of Gov. Solomon Bibo), 129 n. 17, **photo of house**, **88–89**, **90**.
Verde Valley, Ariz., 8 n. 9, 72, 103, 105, **photo en route**, **84**.
Volz, Frederick W., Indian trader, 135, 147 n. 12.
Voth, Rev. Heinrich R., 142, **photo of**, **99**.
Vroman, Adam Clark, Pasadena, Calif., photographer, 118, 128 n. 9, 132, 148 n. 14, **photo by**, **88–89**.

Walker, Aldace F., 147 n. 9.
Walker, J. W., 137.
Walnut Canyon National Monument (Ariz.), 103, 112 n. 10.
Walpi, First Mesa (Hopi), 119; Snake Dance (see also Snake legend), 130, 149 n. 29; **photos of**, **96–100**.
Welles Family genealogy, 3.
Welles, Charles Fisher (paternal grandfather of Amelia and Josephine), 3.
Welles, George, 3–4.
Welles, Gideon, 3, 7 n. 6.
Welles, John Roset (see John Welles Hollenback).
Welles, Thomas, 4.
Welles, Virginia (Mrs. Edward Welles), 7 n. 5.
Wheeler, I. F., 57 n. 9.
Wiki, Antelope Society priest, 142, 149 n. 35.
Wilcox, Elias S., liveryman, 72, 74 n. 16, 72, 74 n. 16, 133, 137, 147 n. 8, **photo of**, **96**; and Viola, 106, 112 n. 13.
Wilkes-Barre (Pa.), 4, 19 n. 4, 126.
Wittick, George Ben, photographer, 132, 135, 139–140, 147 n. 11, 148 n. 25, 149 n. 27; **photo of**, **100**, **photo by**, **99**.
Women, attire, 50, 53, 56 n. 2, 58 n. 16, 72 n. 4; photographers, 19; tourists (see also Ayer, Bass, Cameron, Dox, Doyle, Dutton, Hall, Sturgis, Knox, Thurber) 41, 70, 72 n. 4, 133.
Wyoming Valley (Pa.), 13, 19 n. 4.

Zuni Pueblo (N.M.), 113–114, 119, 124, **photos of**, **93**, **94**.
Zuni Point (see also Bissell Point), 54.